Erica's Blog:

A Tool Kit for Fixing What's Not Working in Your Life

Kendra Brown, PhD and Pat Austin Novak

BALBOA.
PRESS

A DIVISION OF HAY HOUSE

Balboa Press books may be ordered through booksellers or by contacting:

Balboa Press
A Division of Hay House
1663 Liberty Drive
Bloomington, IN 47403
www.balboapress.com
1 (877) 407-4847

Print information available on the last page.

ISBN: 978-1-5043-8936-5 (sc)
ISBN: 978-1-5043-8938-9 (hc)
ISBN: 978-1-5043-8937-2 (e)

Library of Congress Control Number: 2017915290

Balboa Press rev. date: 10/17/2017

Contents

Introduction— Using the Tools

How can people who are otherwise very intelligent find themselves totally confused and frustrated by relationships? Take Erica for example. Although she is fictional, her problems are real and all too common. Erica knows that, while her life isn't bad, it's far from perfect. She repeats the same behaviors and keeps getting the same annoying results: relationships that just don't quite work. She realizes that she needs help getting to the root causes of her difficulties and developing strategies for long-term personal growth.

The self-help articles and books she reads and the friends she consults seem well-intended, but ineffective – sometimes even counter-productive - when she tries to put their advice into practice. She realizes she would benefit from professional advice but hesitates, fearing it could be time consuming or financially prohibitive.

Erica finds a therapist whose philosophy of guided self-help is a good fit. Dr. Kathy's sessions are just what Erica was seeking: she begins to understand her own behaviors and builds a personal "tool kit" full of strategies that she practices as homework and later reviews and "tweaks" with Kathy. The tools include techniques proven effective in numerous settings over many years. They're derived from Transactional Analysis and other cognitive-behavioral theories, mindful meditation, and the Myers-Briggs Personality Indicator. Erica is empowered to look realistically at her own behaviors: discarding, changing, and modifying them so that she can achieve her personal goals.

The tools are not just for Erica, of course. As Erica is learning about them from Dr. Kathy, they are also provided for you. "Pause Buttons" are introduced – encouraging you to take a break from the action and learn more about the tools. Dr. Brown provides in-depth information about each one. Then, you can return to Erica to see how she copes with her new insights and strategies. She doesn't effortlessly and immediately succeed. She finds that "practice makes better – not perfect." If you feel a kinship with Erica, you may be motivated to use the tools too, perhaps comparing your results to hers.

You may, of course, simply enjoy following the delightful Erica and laugh with her as she gains understanding of her behaviors. You can always return later to study the tools.

So, if I'm so smart, why do I keep doing such stupid things?

Relationships for me are like video games where I can't get past the basic levels. I jump, I dodge, I evade the monsters, but I still don't seem to move forward. Did someone hand out an instruction manual and forget to give me one?

I want the manual! I want to know how to deal with my mother without anger or tears, my sister without the need to scream, and my coworkers without resentment over how easily they seem to handle themselves. And I want a long-term relationship with a wonderful man.

And speaking of men, here's the latest on that front. It's not pretty. Last week, I had to explain to the doctor at the walk-in clinic how a fishhook got into my shoulder instead of into a fish—and I swear he smirked before he assured me I was in no danger of tetanus. I'm left with a small scar and some embarrassing memories. And being snared by the fishhook wasn't the worst of it. The really stupid thing was to go fishing in the first place, especially in terrible heat, on an uncomfortable boat, with too much beer and not enough water to drink. Why did I do it? Okay, *this* is the worst part: I did it for a guy, one who wasn't even fun or considerate of me.

Sad to say, my medical history is chock-full of events like this latest one—all in the pursuit of my prince! In thirty-one years, I have sprained an ankle trying to play rugby—rugby! I wasn't even good at field hockey—pulled a hamstring on an advanced trail with a guy who loved to hike, and bruised my hip skiing a slope that was way too tough for me. And now I have a scar on my shoulder from the fishing trip. It seems I have lots of memories of the perils of being a good sport for some guy. Not even *the* guy; just a guy.

Before I lose a limb and whatever is left of my self-esteem, I've got to make a course correction. I'm drawn to guys who have just one huge attraction: they're available! I get kind of desperate, no thanks to my mother and her concern about her single daughter growing overripe on the vine instead of marrying and producing grandkids. Does she really need more baby photos on her cell phone to share with friends?

If I'm being honest, my unhappiness with my life isn't just about guys. Oh yes, there's my mother—like a swirl of emotionally charged free-floating radicals—affecting my mental health when I least expect it!

And work. I'm hurt to the core that I didn't get the promotion I think I truly deserved. What happened? The opportunity was just hanging there, ready for me to pluck like a shiny apple, and I ended up with applesauce. Where is the fairness in the world?

Okay, no one wants to come to my pity party, not even me anymore. I've started this blog as a way of writing myself into action. I have to break the cycle of stupidity in my relationships—or lack of them. Looks like I'll be spending more time on my laptop and less time at singles bars.

Did I mention that otherwise I'm fairly smart? I recently reframed my college diploma to remind myself of that. So I hereby assign myself some homework: check out some of the books that promise their readers will become desirable, happy, rich, tall, thin, sensual, and in touch with the outer rings of Saturn on a really good day! Then I will record in this blog what I'm learning and the progress I'm making.

Maybe I'll meet a guy at the bookstore who's into novels. How much physical damage can I do if we just download books together?

July 5

I've learned I'm not alone in feeling like my life is not on the right trajectory. There are shelves and shelves of self-help books in the bookstore and too many online for human comprehension. Just skimming the titles made me feel better since I'm obviously not seriously mentally ill - although I must admit it's tempting to believe I'm not my mother's daughter! So that takes care of a few shelves.

In the face of so many general guidebooks to happier living, I realize I need to define my problems specifically. Frankly, my irritations seem pale in comparison to some of the subtitles and chapter headings I've skimmed.

All I need for perfection is an ideal man, a powerful yet satisfying career, plenty of money, charming children, and dear friends. And while I'm at it, I might as well throw in world peace, the end to hunger, environmental sustainability, and a size-four body that resists wrinkles. Are there apps for those?

Okay, this is my blog; I'm allowed to be silly and sarcastic now and again. Seriously, though, look at that list I just created. It starts with "an ideal man." Why do I do that? It can't start with a man. Even before I plunge into this stack of reading material, I know that it has to start with me, and unfortunately I'll need to work on relationships all around—with my family and at work, for instance.

So I've got lots of green Thai tea on hand, some multigrain crackers as a slight bow to good nutrition, and a stack of books that all have something in them about self-actualization.

I'll be like a Transformer: watch me turn into a new and improved self in several easy steps.

July 15

Ten days of reading and munching crackers surely has resulted in my gaining pounds but no noticeable increase in wisdom for my psyche. How do I know this for sure? Because I've just done some of the same stupid things I did before reading all those books.

Yes, dear reader, I went out with *him*. We have nothing in common—he's even a bit rude—but I started talking to him outside the bookstore (he was heading for the sporting goods store, of course), and I jumped at the chance for a date. To a hockey game. And he met me inside, which meant that I paid my own way. At least I didn't have to pay his admission too. Mostly, he ignored me while he yelled and jumped out of his seat and ordered beer. On the way out, he seemed to expect that we'd be going back to my place or his. What on earth was I thinking?

This dreadful date was followed by a conversation with my mother about the charmed life my sister is leading, what a great wife she is, and how nice it would be if I were settled too. The conversation ended as it usually does: with my being sarcastic with her and then crying to myself.

So all this reading and no transformation.

July 16

I checked my company's benefits plan to see if mental health services are covered.

If I get committed to a mental institution, I'm in good shape. As I understand the policy, if I simply go to a therapist, most of the charges will be my responsibility. I don't suppose that, since I have really good teeth, I could trade some of the company's dental coverage for therapy? I'm too embarrassed to even ask the human resources people to clarify the benefits. And I don't know any therapists. What if the therapist doesn't have the answers I need? Then I'd still be clueless—and in debt!

Well, I've got a few more self-help books on my nightstand, and some magazines that promise to change my personality and guide me to my best new hairstyle as a bonus. I've got my fingers crossed that they will unlock the secrets to my transformation. Stay tuned.

July 21

Serendipity. I love the word, and I just experienced it.

I'm frustrated and tired after reading so many self-help books and make-yourself-over magazine articles. They seem helpful while I'm reading them, but the recommendations just don't stick once I've put them down and gotten back into the reality of my everyday life. Okay, so what I want is to implant all that wisdom directly into my brain, like an instant download. Then I can replay their words over and over in my brain before I do the next stupid thing.

But back to serendipity.

I was reading a local magazine proclaiming that this city is the best place in the world to live. (Ah, the joys of perfect lighting and Photoshop!) This month's issue featured a local therapist who has a new niche: she provides psycho-education to clients who can only afford short-term therapy. Clients must be willing to do homework on their own with the help of strategies and techniques she provides. She calls them tool kits. Her therapy is for clients dealing with specific life obstacles and not for those struggling with serious mental health issues.

This is just the kind of practical approach I've been hoping for—and it fits my budget! I can picture it now: takeaway tools to fix yourself when you're having minor breakdowns on the road or when you're transforming yourself and some piece doesn't twist the way it's supposed to.

I've got a phone number, an address, a website, a Facebook page, and a good feeling about this. I just hope that she is what she seems to be. And I hope I make that phone call.

July 31

I didn't make the call. My friend Lisa gave me one more out. She said I didn't need a therapist, just a good friend to talk to over lunch.

So I bought her lunch. And I admit that she did listen while I talked, which is more than you can get from most people. She agreed with me on every point: men are jerks, life is cruel, my mother is a giant pain, my sister got all the breaks, and no one at work appreciates me. But other than a charge on my credit card, I didn't really get much more out of it.

How do I know? Because I had another fight with my mother, both of us turning into adolescent brats with each other. Telling my friend how easily and often this happens didn't do anything to prevent it from happening again. None of Lisa's well-meaning advice worked because her relationship with her mom just isn't the same as mine.

Mom means well, I know that. She wants me to be happily married and settled, having children with a guy who earns enough so that I can stay home and take care of the kids. Mom still regrets having to work full-time during my childhood to keep the family afloat. I know it's her wishing the best for me, but I just can't pull it off. I feel defeated and conflicted; part of me wants to be in a loving dialogue with Mom, and the other Erica gets belligerent to ward off her one-size-fits-all solution.

So on Thursday, she called to tell me about my sister's latest and greatest family stories. I'm glad for my sister and for Mom. Really, I am. But what I heard underneath all of this was, "Too bad I can't say the same about you."

I started contradicting everything she said except for "Hello." By the time we stopped talking, I tossed my phone on the table and just narrowly missed immersing it in my dinner. I'm sure my sister had a lovely home-cooked, nutritionally balanced, beautifully presented meal on her table. I had canned soup.

The truth is that even though I want some of those things for myself, I'm not really intent on staying home instead of working. While it's not politically correct to admit this at work, I like my job. I do want a husband and children, but I also want to continue with my career. Put all of that together, and it makes a terrific package—an American-dream sort of thing.

If it's going to happen, I guess I need more help than just having lunch with a friend. I swear I'll make the call.

August 6

Meeting one—or session one (working on my psychology vocabulary here!). Dr. Johnson ("Call me Kathy, please.") is the therapist's name, and she is a cognitive-behavioral psychologist. She explained that her focus is on helping clients identify and change current behaviors that are causing problems, as well as the thoughts and emotions linked to these behaviors.

I'm already feeling a bit more at ease. First of all, the waiting room is decorated in soothing colors with attractive art. It smells nice, and there weren't any people hanging about who seemed out of touch with reality.

Of course, I couldn't just wait until she started talking. I had to go first. I wanted her to know I read her article, I didn't have insurance for this sort of thing, I only wanted a little help with a few issues, and I didn't expect to see her more than a couple of times.

I'm not sure how she did it, but she made me feel as if that were all fine, instead of letting me know that I was a complete boor who should have duct tape over my mouth.

Then she started asking me questions—very specific questions and some of them, to me, totally outlandish: Was there a history of abusive behavior in my family or other relationships? Were there any times when I was abusive? Any patterns of mood swings? Is there a history of substance abuse? Do I have any symptoms of serious anxiety or depression?

I felt as if I was being psychoanalyzed. Oh wait, that's exactly what I wanted! Figure me out, please. Make it all better.

Kathy explained that her questions were part of a clinical

assessment, making sure that her therapy and my issues were a good match. Apparently my assessment added up to "relatively healthy." That's a relief. According to Kathy, the kind of supervised self-help program I want from her wouldn't be a good match if I had serious problems. In that case, I'd need ongoing, in-depth therapy.

Then she gave me homework: I have to make pies! Thank goodness these aren't the ones I've looked at longingly in Mom's cookbooks, where you begin by learning how to make never-fail French pastry. My baked goods always come from someone else's home or the local bakery.

The pies I'm making are similar to the pie charts we analyze at budget meetings. I'm supposed to draw a circle for each problem area that I want to work on and then—oh, this is going to be good!—determine how much of the pie I'm responsible for and how much someone else is responsible for.

I hadn't thought of these problems as having distinct segments. They've always seemed to be more like big clumps of twisty things. But okay, here goes—analysis time.

Pause Button

Tool #1 Finding Your Personal Guide

Erica has (reluctantly, I admit) sought the help of a therapist. Her psychologist, Dr. Kathy Johnson, decided that Erica was a suitable client for her therapy based on a clinical assessment. Please look back at the questions Kathy asked Erica. If your response to any of those questions is yes, I strongly urge you to work with a therapist who has expertise in those areas.

Regardless of your assessment, if you decide to seek therapy, I encourage you to make sure the therapist is a licensed mental health professional, not simply a person who advertises her- or himself as certified. Psychiatrists, psychologists, clinical social workers, marriage and family therapists, and pastoral counselors are rigorously trained professionals. They have been tested with state and national exams and must comply with ethical standards. Training in these professions involves many years and is scrutinized by various boards. When you seek the help of a therapist, be sure that professional is licensed by your state to treat mental health issues. Interview them about their degrees and years of training. After all, if you only needed well-intended advice, you could ask a friend!

August 9

Pie day!

I got out some really nice unlined paper, some multicolored sharpies, and started making pies by tracing around a pie pan (of course!) to make sure that they were perfect circles.

The first pie was Mother. The second one: guys. The third one was my sister, Laura. And since I was getting good at tracing these pie shapes, I made a few more: work and boss, along with an abstract one (dreams for the future) and a silly one (my hair and freckles).

I stopped before I built a whole pie shop.

Feeling oh-so in command, I drew up a color key, figuring I'd get extra points for having such classy-looking pies. My slivers of the pies will be yellow, while my mother's will be blue (luckily, I have two blue markers on hand since I may need a lot of that color!). My sister's color can be pink, which she'd like very much—*so* feminine. Guys are red, work will be green, and I have a fuchsia marker for my boss.

So far, lots of fun. Then, I hit a wall. If Pie One represents all my problems with my mother, can I really color the whole thing blue? It dawned on me right away that I was going to have to color some slivers with my yellow pen if I'm being really honest.

I almost tossed the pies. This was not fun after all.

I spent the whole evening on one pie, mostly staring at the shape and getting weepy—partly out of self-pity, but also a bit out of embarrassment at how judgmental I've been toward my mother, while I've been overly forgiving of my father and oblivious to my own responsibility for the problems in my relationship with Mom.

I almost called her to apologize, but she wouldn't understand this bit about pies, and knowing me, I'd probably get annoyed at something she said and we'd be back in the thick of it. No, I decided to turn in my homework to Kathy first.

Pause Button

Tool #2 Making Your Own Pie

On a blank sheet of paper, draw a circle to represent the outline of a pie (you don't have to make them perfect like Erica!).

Think of someone with whom you have a difficult relationship. Write that person's name above the pie.

Take a few minutes to sit back and really reflect on your typical conflicts or unpleasant interactions with this person. You'll get the best results from this exercise if you:

1. Set aside ten to fifteen minutes for this important exercise.
2. Pick a quiet place to do it, away from phones, TV, and other distractions.
3. Think of a general pattern or typical conflicts, or select a specific event.

You may see and hear many details as you examine this pie. It may surprise you to observe the internal drama that takes place in your brain's theater when you become your own audience. (By the way, this is a tool in itself, which will be discussed in more detail later in Tool #6, the meditation called Snowflakes.)

Now, having listened and observed, divide the pie up into slices. What portion of the pie is the fault of that difficult other? What portion belongs to other people who play some role in this conflict? Finally, what portion of the pie is yours? Don't skip this important part of the exercise. After all, your portion is the part of the pie you can most directly and effectively change. On the other hand, don't claim too much of the pie for yourself, thus omitting the parts that others play in creating this unsavory dish.

You now have a rough picture of this problem pie. It will be even more helpful if you add descriptors and details in each portion. Here are two examples—either one could be an accurate assessment, depending on the situation:

(1) "I have this much of the pie because I never speak up for myself with this person. I'm afraid of his anger, and I keep being nice no matter how he treats me!"

(2) "John gets the majority of this pie. He is such an angry person and speaks so loudly when he argues that it scares me! Other people also experience this with John. Their results aren't any better than mine, no matter how they respond to him."

When we're honest about the composition of our problem pies, we often discover that these ineffective interactions are much more complex than we previously thought. And once we see them more accurately, we may find new ways to behave—new strategies and solutions. We can change our portions of the pie. When this occurs, we often find the whole pie changes, just as changing an ingredient in a pie recipe alters the final product!

To summarize the recipe:

1. Take some time. You are worth it.
2. Draw the basic pie shape.
3. Reflect on the conflict(s) that makes this a problem pie for you.

4. Divide the pie into slices.

5. Add descriptors.

6. Keep the pie picture handy. You'll want to notice changes!

August 13

No matter how old I get, I don't think I'll ever lose that horrible sensation of turning in a paper to a teacher and waiting for the verdict.

Kathy seemed amused by my color-coding, which made my pie with Mom look like it was tie-dyed. There was no verdict, though, just some gentle prodding to help me get through a session that turned out to be a lot more difficult for me than I'd expected.

For the first time, I admitted to myself that I crave my mother's approval. Why then have I pushed her away and argued with her and defied everything she says? Funny way to win approval, huh? But as I was coloring in the blue sections to be sure I kept the focus on Mom and her lack of appreciation for me, I found myself reaching for a bit of brown to represent my dad's part of this conflicted pie.

He was everything to me and everything I wanted to be: smart, active in our community, and busy doing interesting things. Dad always had time for anything fun. I idolized him.

But he also drank to excess. Funny, at the time, nobody in the family talked about it. We all just accepted it as part of life and still seem to see it that way. I guess all kids do that, no matter how normal or awful the situation is. It's what they know. I've heard friends talk about ignoring the elephant in the room—as if it didn't exist. Come to think about it, I do have a real talent for ignoring bad behaviors, especially in males. I think I'm onto something here, even if it is unpleasant.

Dad was always my hero, and to be honest, more of a playmate than a parent. He always called on me to be on his side in his arguments with my mother. "Put up the storm windows? Erica, your mother wants me to spend this beautiful day putting up the storm windows. Don't you think we should take the canoe down to the park for a last ride before it gets too cold?" Of course I did. So we went, and Mom, who worked all week just like Dad, put up the storm windows while we were canoeing. As I got older, I was always his designated driver when we went out for one of our adventures together. I liked the feeling of being responsible for my father.

Multiply this scene dozens of times—I can't bear to catalog them— and they are all throughout my childhood.

Then he died.

That swirl of pink in the pie is my sister, staying loyal to my mother and, if my dad were still alive, she'd probably be in the same kind of relationship with him that I'm in with my mom.

Kathy helped me see that we all share in the responsibility for a conflicted relationship. I want to stop playing the part of angry daughter, disappointed employee, disappointing sister, and girl on the edge of a fulfilling life. I want to make it better. I really do.

So where's the nicely phrased solution to this problem, please, dear psychologist?

Kathy didn't answer my unspoken question. All she said was that I was really making progress, and she assigned more pie-making for homework!

August 20

Oh, today wasn't a comfortable session! We began by reviewing my collection of pies. I had an impressive portfolio because I'd spent a lot of time on them. When I finished looking at my current problem relationships, I went back and revisited some from my past.

I gave myself high marks for the numbers of pies, but I was

dismayed at the amount of yellow I saw before me as I placed them in front of Kathy. She, on the other hand, seemed pleased with the yellow spread! She said that I'm starting to understand that I have a lot more responsibility for harmony or problems in my relationships than I was willing to admit before I started these sessions.

Kathy challenged me to ask myself a couple of questions each time I analyze one of my pies: "Which pieces of this pie can I directly affect?" and "Where can I, personally, make or influence a change?" These are the questions of the moment.

Well, I can't change my mother, that's for sure. But I get where Kathy is pushing me. I can change my own behavior. That's my main job, and I know it now. But, there is some good news: It seems I can indirectly change other people's behavior when I change my own. Of course I've experienced this in situations where there's not much at stake. Everyone knows that, usually, you get better service in a store or restaurant when you are nice to the staff. So, I need to stop complaining about my mother and change my behavior when I'm with her. Easier said than done.

Now, there is a big part of me that doesn't want to give up my version of "Who caused this anyway?" It was so much easier to see my mother as the lone villain in the Mom pie, or my boss as the bad guy. Kathy said I've made an important step in healing, even if it doesn't feel comfortable yet.

Just as I was getting the hang of pie-making, Kathy introduced a new tool. She wants me to understand that many tools she uses are from the work of Dr. Eric Berne, Dr. Thomas Harris, Dr. Franklin Ernst, and many other transactional analysts. It seems important to Kathy that I understand the tools she'll be teaching me are her abbreviated and personalized versions of their theories—modified to work for her. I wrote down these names so I can Google them later if needed.

Kathy asked me to look at a chart she calls the Four Life Positions. She gave me several copies of the chart because I'll be using them for homework (the woman is relentless!). She pointed out the various positions and said she often compares them to diving platforms from which we leap into situations. She said that, from childhood, we make conclusions of self-worth based on how we perceive others who are important to us and how we feel or think they reacted to us. She asked that I look at the chart and see if I can figure out which positions I occupied as a child and as a young adult, and which positions are typical for me now.

Here are the positions on the chart:

I'm OK/You're OK
I'm OK/You're Not OK
I'm Not OK/You're OK
I'm Not OK/You're Not OK

Kathy emphasized that these positions are about being **OK** or **Not OK,** and that an important part of this tool is to realize that "OK" means just what is says: You're okay, not perfect. That means I can have some flaws. I can do foolish things sometimes. I can have strong points, as well as pockets of stupidity. Yet I can still be basically acceptable. I can still be okay.

I was surprised at my response to this new idea that we are all slightly irregulars. It seems to me that it should be comforting; actually, it's kind of hard to accept. I want to excel. I thought that the goal was to be perfect, or pretty close to it. I can be okay? I don't have to be absolutely perfect all the time? Huh!

I can see right away that "I'm OK/You're OK" is the best position.

That's where I want to be. And I want to be there all the time. Yep, aiming for perfection, as usual.

Just to be sure I understood this tool from transactional analysis, Kathy asked about my relationship with Dad. What position would describe our interactions? Well, that was easy! I saw Dad as easy and fun. And we got along really well. I felt that he enjoyed my company. I could easily see that with respect to Dad, we land on the "I'm OK/ You're OK" platform. Whew! That place feels good.

But I was already dreading the next question: How about you and Mom?

I was so ready to give her the answer to show I'm getting it! But, then, she didn't ask. Instead, she assigned me homework. I'm to pay close attention to the positions I'm taking with others in my everyday life, especially with Mom, my sister, and my boss. I've attached a copy of the chart to my refrigerator as a daily reminder to check out my positions.

It'll take me a while to get the hang of it. Right now I'm not feeling as if I'm OK. And if the pie inventory wasn't enough, Kathy asked that I report my observations and insights from the Life Positions chart in our next session. This therapy stuff is no piece of cake! Sorry, I couldn't resist that. I'm on a roll!

All right, enough about bakery items—lots of homework ahead. Kathy says some people find keeping a journal of these discoveries is helpful. I told her about you, my newest companion, Dear Blog, and she seemed to think you are a very good idea. I won't see Kathy again for two weeks, so I'll have lots of time for my homework.

Note to self: Here are the original source documents for future reference:

Games People Play by Eric Berne, MD
I'm OK—You're OK by Thomas Harris, MD
TA Today by Ian Stewart and Vann Joines
Transactional Analysis in the OK Corral: Grid for What's Happening by Dr. Franklin H. Ernst, Jr.
Tony White. "Life Positions." *Transactional Analysis Journal* 24, no. 4 (October 1994): 269–276.

Pause Button

Tool #3 Developing a Life-Positions Chart of Your Own

Set aside about ten to twenty minutes so you can reflect quietly on relationships with important people in your life, either current ones or those from the past.

Divide an 8 ½ x 11 sheet of paper into four equal boxes. Label one box (for convenience, let's call that Position 1) "I'm OK/You're OK." Label the next box (Position 2) "I'm Not OK/You're OK." Label the third box (Position 3) "I'm OK/You're Not OK." And the final box (Position 4) "I'm Not OK/You're Not OK." Most of us have experienced these positions at one time or another in our lives, or we may experience each of them routinely, depending on our daily interactions.

As you examine these four positions, does one of them stand out to you as more familiar? Let's start with Position 1. As Kathy pointed out, it's more pleasant to be in "I'm OK/You're OK." For example, you may feel pleasure as you think of time spent with a special friend. When you are with this person, you feel accepted. You can be yourself. You don't feel defensive. And you don't feel critical. You probably have lots of fun together and laugh easily. You could write that person's name in the "I'm OK/You're OK" box and describe how you feel and what you do when you're together. Someone once described her experience with her spouse as, "When I'm with him, I can live out loud!" That's definitely a feeling that comes out of the "I'm OK/You're OK" position.

Now, let's look at position 2: "I'm Not OK/You're OK." This is a very familiar position in childhood for many people. When you were a child, did you feel inferior and unloved by one of your parents or some other significant person? Were you always trying (often in vain) to please that person? If so, you may recall how it felt (or still feels) to be in that position: feeling unaccepted and routinely desiring the approval of that important person. Make a note of the people in your life who enhance the chances you will find yourself in that box.

It's obvious, by the way, that at least to some extent we are all familiar with this position. As children, even if we had thoughtful, nurturing parents, we were relatively powerless and ineffective compared to our parental and authority figures. We lacked their wisdom, strength, and ability to be self-sufficient. Thus, to varying degrees, depending on many factors, we can all identify with this box.

As for Position 3: It may occur to you that when you're around some people, you often have to bite your tongue to resist criticizing their choices and behaviors. You may have described them (at least to yourself) as incompetent or lazy. You wouldn't trust them to complete a task—you'd rather just do it yourself! This is "I'm OK/ You're Not OK." It's important to be sensitive to this position when we are helping someone less capable or fortunate than we are. Our goal—if we want the person to succeed—is to empower him or her, to help the person feel "I'm OK/You're OK."

The last position, "I'm Not OK/You're Not OK," is the least positive position of all. When you're in this position, you are assuming that neither you nor the other person is competent (okay). This box is sometimes described as the hopeless and helpless position. Nobody seems to have power to overcome obstacles or accomplish goals. Sometimes people express these feelings when dealing with a large entity, such as the government, as in, "You can't fight City Hall!"

Dr. Franklin Ernst developed an impressive model about these kinds of social interactions and published them in his work about the OK Corral (see reference). As he and other transactional analysts pointed out, we may identify one of these positions as our primary one from childhood. As we mature, events and relationships (both good and bad) can alter how we view ourselves and others. Even so, we may often revert to earlier familiar positions when we are under stress.

There are two pieces of good news: One, our positions vis-à-vis others are fluid, rather than static or fixed; and two, the changes we make in our own behaviors can influence the nature of our relationships with those around us. We can change the quality of interactions with others by noticing where we are standing—that is, what position are we assuming when we engage with this or that person. When we move to a more positive position, we will often get a more positive result.

If this tool is helpful for you, you may enjoy keeping a series of charts that show how your relationships with specific others are changing or have changed. So, for example, if you always avoided a confrontation with your best friend—trying to please her, from the "I'm Not OK/You're OK" position—you might move into the "I'm OK/You're OK" position and try being more quietly assertive. If this is successful (and it often is), you may marvel that you feel better about yourself and her. Keeping notes about these changes will reinforce what you are learning and encourage you to continue your progress.

As you will see from the following experiences told by Erica, sometimes our changes have good results, and sometimes they don't. There are even times when people are simply not able to join us in "I'm OK/You're OK."

September 3

I can't believe I'm such a product of my past. I'm so used to thinking that a new school year starts right around Labor Day that even now, years after graduating, I still feel as though this time of year marks a new beginning.

I sure wish all I needed to do was buy fresh pencils and a themed lunch box to get started on a new adventure with these positioning statements. Oops, how old-fashioned—pencils. I, of course, would be getting a new laptop, or tablet, in a snazzy case that expressed my unique personality.

In our office, where most everything zips from person to person electronically, we still have copy machine wars. Right before a meeting, you can depend on it. There will be people jostling to get to the copier so they can come into the meeting with stacks of paper. Quantity counts.

As usual, the copier ran out of paper just before I got my turn. I was furious. In the copy wars, the first person who comes along post-paper has the right to be bitter, angry, sarcastic, and all-around annoying. Okay, I'm trying out the positioning thing, so instead of assuming that no one else is okay, especially the fools in front of me who used up all the paper and didn't replace it, I decided to pretend that we're all okay. I laughed and made some joke, put paper in the machine, and told the person behind me that it was now okay to copy *War and Peace* because I added enough paper for all the Russian novelists from two centuries.

Everyone laughed. I felt great—smug even—that I had chosen to be my better self, my "I'm okay, you're okay, even the copier is okay" self. The results were astounding. During the meeting, people around the table actually deferred to me at points in the discussion. My input was treated as though I had just ingested the Dali Lama. Someone even got me a cup of coffee! I didn't want coffee, but it felt nice to be treated with such respect.

Afterward, though, I felt a bit like a fake. I didn't really think everyone was okay. I wanted to scream at the coward who slunk away when the paper ran out. But Kathy assures me that "it's okay to fake it until you make it." She said this slogan, from the program of Alcoholics Anonymous, has helped many people work on improving their relationships and their own behaviors, and many of Kathy's clients say it's a handy tool in all kinds of situations.

I like the results. I like the feeling that I am in control of my emotions and that other people value me. If I were a scheming person, I could see how using this position could be very helpful in life, even if your innermost cells are screaming, "You're not OK; no one's OK." This experience with the four positions was really successful and amazing. When I acted as if all of us were okay, we really were.

September 4

Fate has an interesting way of pulling me up short and reminding me that I'm not quite as great as I thought.

So I'm cruising along today, satisfied that I've got this positioning thing mastered, at least in the position that I know is the right answer to every question, when I made a fool of myself and found myself in what I call Position Number 2 (I'm not OK, but you're OK). It's just as awful as you would expect Number 2 to be.

When Jake in Accounting stormed into my office this morning, waving a budget sheet at me, I caved before I even knew what he was flapping at me or why I should care. I think he studied management techniques on Mount Vesuvius: when in doubt, erupt. He intimidates me. Partly it's his personality; partly it's because he always seems to have numbers on his side.

Today, he erupted at me because I hadn't included the allocated overhead on one of our projects. I immediately assumed that he was right, and I had made a huge error. So wouldn't you think I would simply say to him, "I'm so sorry. I'll fix that this afternoon"? And everyone's okay.

No, as I could feel myself hurtling toward the deep abyss in which I am totally not okay. How stupid of me. How irresponsible. I mumbled something incoherent and then hid in my office until I could compose myself.

I'm learning that when I feel threatened or angry or fearful, I become sarcastic as a defense. I didn't feel okay, and so when I went out for lunch, I snapped at the person behind the sandwich counter who couldn't seem to understand what "no mayonnaise" meant. Since I wasn't okay, I made sure someone else felt not okay. How petty of me.

If I were making one of those annoying pies right now, I'd want to color the whole thing burnt umber—the color I've chosen for Mr. Accounting. I'd like to blame him. Thanks to Kathy, though, I realize that, in his annoying way, he was simply being who he is and doing his job. It's my reaction of buying into his implication that I'm not OK that set things off badly.

So now the pie goes dark, like my mood. It's me; I'm the problem. Will I ever learn?

September 10

A new day, and I'm determined to try out this positioning stuff with my sister, keeping in mind some of the things Kathy has taught me: I'm OK, I really am. If I can just remember that and watch my own behavior, as well as my sister's, we might both feel okay.

I keep thinking of the phrase: "The triumph of hope over experience." I hope that's not going to be the theme of the day because we're taking her seven-year-old daughter shopping.

Later.

So, not so bad. My older niece, Carlene, is really cute, and we had a good time in the children's clothing section. She tried on outfits "just like a big girl," and who could not enjoy her look of absolute trust in my judgment as to whether the sparkles were bright enough, and whether the duck shirt was more perfect than the frog one? We took lots of pictures and messaged them to her best friend, who gave her the okay.

What was totally amazing, though, was how well I got along with my sister. We started trading stories about the clothes my mother made us wear when we were young—always a collared shirt, when any self-respecting second grader would wear a tee shirt with a princess or a cartoon character on it; sensible shoes, when what we really wanted were the cheap sparkly ones in red or silver; and perfect-looking jeans instead of a pair with artistically placed holes and shredded edges.

For a while, we were both okay because we were allied against Mom, who was not okay, but in a very mild way. We talked about her behaviors, without antagonism, as a cherished kind of nuttiness.

It's a start at least. We need to relate better even when we don't have a cute kid as a foil and when we're not reminiscing. Still, I respect the way my sister treated her daughter. We didn't argue over clothes, diet, or relationships! We both left with the sense that this had been a good day.

September 12

I wonder if this "You're OK" position has its limits. Today I came up against someone who definitely seems to be less than okay in my view, and I don't think that I'm the problem this time.

I took my car for an oil change. Congratulations are in order, please. I did it on time, thanks to a message on my phone that reminded me. There was an older man in the waiting room where a television was blasting some talk show. The guy screamed—literally screamed—at the TV with really abusive, embarrassing language. I tried to disappear into a magazine, a two-year-old copy of *Field and Stream*, so you know how desperate I felt. Suddenly, he turned on me and began hurling epithets about women and the way they've taken over the world (Oh, if that were so!) and ruined everything for men like him. He started to get in my face.

Would Kathy want me to try to reposition this situation so that we were in the "I'm OK/You're OK" mode? No, I think not. This guy was just not okay. I chose the strategy of getting out of there. You'd be amazed at how fascinating the posters in a car dealership corridor can be if you entirely focus on them in order to block out the raging bull in the waiting room.

So now I'm reflecting. I've just looked at some notes I took during my last session with Kathy. They are really making sense to me now. I must be learning this stuff! "Sometimes there's nothing I can do except remember that I'm OK. Keeping out of the way of someone who's not okay can be a strategy."

I can't make too much out of this incident. It's not typical of my life, and it doesn't resolve any of my problems with people close to me. But that man was an example of someone who will just never fit in my preferred corner of "I'm OK/You're OK."

September 15

Really, I'm amazed at what I'm learning! Before Kathy made me so conscious of positions and pies and where I fit in relation to the people in my life, I would have said emphatically that my problems start with my assumption that I'm not okay—and others are okay.

Wrong.

Now that I'm observing my own behavior, I find myself annoying! I am more likely to assume that I'm fine, whereas the people around me are all jerks, so I act accordingly. I'm often in the "I'm OK/You're Not OK" position—what a surprise!

Today I got into a discussion with one of my coworkers about a project that has been a challenge for our team, but an interesting one. She's not the brightest among us, and I hate the slow way she talks. She worked all weekend on solutions to one of our problems and drew a diagram of how she thought we could keep all of our stakeholders engaged while important documents were written.

How can anyone who talks so slowly produce good work—and work that may be better than mine? I assumed that she couldn't and that her efforts would be the product of a simple mind, so I was condescending to her, telling her that perhaps a junior member of the department could take her work and turn it into a spreadsheet that we could all understand. I'm *so* okay. I made her feel so *not* okay.

Oh, Erica, will you ever learn?

Message to self: how easy it is to assume things about other people and to relish the idea that you're superior to them. I intend to talk to her first thing in the morning, praise her initiative, ask if I can see what she's got so far, and then see if her ideas can work. Most of all, I will treat her from the "I'm OK/You're OK" position. And I swear, really I do, that I will not grit my teeth when she talks slowly. It's okay.

An interruption: I'm still thinking of my dad, and how we got along so well, and how different it has always been with me and my mom. It's as though we're on parallel escalators. I think my mom and I are side by side, and so we're in sync. But the minute we try to talk about anything important, we're in a poor interaction that neither of us can resolve because, after all, our escalators are parallel. We're in the same positions relative to each other forever. :(

September 22

Now she's got me making snowmen, or, as I corrected her, snowpersons. Let's be gender sensitive here, even if it's only snow.

Kathy started our session by praising me for the work I've been doing on my own and the insights I'm gaining. I love praise. So, just as I was feeling confident with my new skills, she told me she had another potentially useful tool. First, Kathy asked me to take a few minutes and ponder the question: "Who are you?" She emphasized *you.*

Before I had a chance to respond with some data appropriate for the census taker, Kathy asked it differently: "Remember when you met the attractive man outside the bookstore, accepted a date with him, regretted it almost immediately, and fussed at yourself for a week?" How could I forget? "Well," she asked, "Are you the 'you' who was attracted, or the 'you' who regretted, or the 'you' who keeps shaming you?"

Uh-oh, I could see where this was headed. It's just easier to think of myself as one unified, straightforward person. It seems that I am split into different me's (many mini-me's?).

30

Kathy asked that I think about how I became "me." She explained that we are all excellent data collectors. We gather the data consciously and unconsciously. From infancy, we watch important authority figures—like our parents—and see how they treat one another, as well as how they treat us. We hear their rules, values, and beliefs. We store this information. We try different tactics to see how we can get what we want, starting with maybe a favorite toy or a cookie instead of carrots. We collect in memory the coping strategies that seem to work and discard those that don't. The data we collect actually becomes "us" in a way. It guides and directs us, and it shapes our beliefs. This data, Kathy says, has more power than we'd expect because we're not conscious of it. We just think we're being ourselves.

Kathy said she finds it easier to group these data collections into a diagram she borrowed from Dr. Eric Berne and other transactional analysts. Many people find this figure useful to picture the parts of themselves, how those parts guide and direct behavior, and how the parts are often in conflict. She was careful to remind me that her simplified version is not the pure original theory, but it is a way of picturing personality dynamics that works for her and many of her clients.

I watched as Kathy began drawing what a kindergarten kid would recognize right away as a snowman (snowperson!): three circles, one on top of the other. I waited in anticipation, hoping she would have me inserting button eyes and a carrot nose. I couldn't resist commenting that her snowperson wasn't anatomically correct, since the circles were all equal size! Kathy just smiled at me and said this diagram represents Dr. Berne's ego states and that his ego-state therapy could be very helpful and instructive for me.

She asked me to describe my inner dialogue when I'm frustrated at myself for making a mistake. No scarcity of material there! Then

I had to think about the actual sentences I say and who they sound like. I knew immediately that one of my inner voices sounds a lot like Mom! As I thought about the blaming, shaming messages, I noticed that none of them were from my dad. Small surprise, since he was often my playmate and partner in crime. Two parents—two very different relationships.

Kathy directed my attention to the top circle of the diagram. She referred to this section as the Parent part, which she then divided into two parts: a Critical Parent and a Nurturing Parent.

She suggested that during my early life, from birth to about age eighteen, I had been collecting messages about rules—the shoulds and shouldn'ts, the dos and the don'ts, and the standards of behavior that I heard or observed. These rules, judgments, and restrictions were recorded in the Critical Parent of my "self." The behaviors related to comforting and nurturing were recorded in my Nurturing Parent. These Parent messages and rules are often simply accepted without question since we hear them from the authority figures with power and control over our lives.

So, in my two inner Parent parts, I have the rules and also the values I've internalized. There are also lots of how-to messages about everything, from how to manage a budget to when to send thank-you notes.

Obviously, we all need parents to guide us in understanding the world and how we're going to fit into it. Without our Critical Parents, we wouldn't stop at red lights and we would live on brownies. As I think about this part now, though, I imagine that we could easily become overly critical of ourselves and others—maybe trying to lay down the law to them or picking at everything they do that doesn't fit in with how we expect things to be done.

So is that why the voice that keeps telling me how I should be living my life always sounds like my mother?

32

Kathy said when my Critical Parent is too fault-finding, she may even shut down my Nurturing Parent, my internal supporter. And probably just when I need my cheerleader the most. It's hard to be honest about myself when I only hear the droning voice of the faultfinder.

Are these parts sort of like internal computer programs? Kathy said that was a good way to think of them, like the underlying systems programs that we don't think about unless the computer isn't working right.

Then she moved on to the middle circle. She drew a big A there and said that is the Adult part. I jumped to the conclusion that this must be the grown-up part of me, and I wondered out loud when I'll meet her! But Kathy just smiled and said that the Adult was more like an information processor, gathering facts and making decisions, like how many bananas to buy at the grocery store. This Adult part observes the outside world; she notices from a detached standpoint what others are saying and doing. Kathy said that even my little niece Gabrielle at age two has an inner Adult. She uses it to find her toys and learn her daily routine, for example.

Finally, she divided the bottom circle into two parts and asked me to describe Gabrielle. I can't talk about Gabby, as we call her, without laughing. She's so uninhibited and busy nonstop. Kathy asked if it was easy to tell how Gabby is feeling at any particular point in time. Oh, yes. She doesn't hide her feelings or thoughts—out they pop, to our delight most of the time, and to her parents' embarrassment now and then. Kathy said I had just described the Natural Child part of the snowperson.

Too bad you outgrow that, I said, thinking what fun it would be to say exactly what I think and maybe even throw some blocks across the room occasionally.

Kathy reassured me that we don't outgrow that part. It is actually there all of our lives, but that other parts of our "self" suppress it. Along with some help from outsiders, I thought. She explained that we all need some natural child in us. It's our playful side, our natural and uninhibited self. It's where joy and creativity reside. This explains my dad perfectly. I loved how spontaneous he was and how he included me in his adventures.

I noticed we had one part left. Kathy said that was the Adapted Child. She asked if I've noticed Gabby restraining any of her natural urges lately. Well, yes. Usually she goes full tilt across the playground, waiting for no one, and lunges for the ladder to the slide. Last week, though, there was another little girl by the slide who was shyly waiting for her chance to climb the ladder. I noticed Gabby acting like a little mother, encouraging the child to try the bottom step and moving out of the way for her.

Kathy asked that I use this ego-state diagram (I'm still going to call mine a snowperson) and picture the various aspects of Gabby and how they interacted to bring about this change of behavior. I could see what was happening. Gabby's Natural Child wants to run free without restraints of any kind and take full possession of the slide for herself, but her Adult part and both her inner Critical and Nurturing Parent are cautioning her and making her more aware of others. So she restrains herself—she adapts. The Child part of her has to learn coping strategies and become adapted to a life with others, where she can't just do whatever she feels like doing.

My imagination took me from my analysis of Gabby to myself. I have always been compliant with rules. Didn't I always complete all of my workbooks in school? But internally I'm conflicted because what I really want to do is defy authority, run off with my dad, and just have fun. I seethe with anger at anyone who gives me orders or even strong suggestions. I don't show it. I guess that is another adaptation. But it makes me feel very put-upon. Then I become sarcastic and undermine what could be a fine relationship.

I felt sad after this analysis.

Kathy noticed my mood and asked me about it. I was picturing going through life just functioning in the Adult and Critical Parent parts, along with Adapted Child. No fun there! Kathy assured me that all parts are fine and work well together. I just need to become conscious of them and decide which parts are most effective for specific situations. However, unless and until I become aware of all the aspects of my "self," I function as if I'm on automatic pilot.

And then I got a compliment! Kathy said my sadness was actually a positive sign. She said healing can feel scary at times because you are taking risks, stripping away the coping strategies and facades to look honestly at yourself. She encouraged me to think of the process as freeing instead of fearful because I can now pick healthier ways to reach my goals and interact with others. I can also choose to be kinder and less critical to myself.

So okay, it's important to spend some time listening to our Adult part. Give it time to process the information. The Adult gets to be the observer of what's happening. It's not that the Adult is cold and unfeeling exactly. The Adult is a data gatherer—just watching and noting, observing with the goal of understanding how it all fits together. It's the right place for regaining awareness, or consciousness, rather than being dictated to by earlier parental commands or operating from a reactive child position of either rebelling or complying automatically.

Homework again: Besides continuing to observe my own actions and reactions in day-to-day situations, I have a cheat sheet so that I have a practical approach to all of the theories that Kathy just gave me.

My homework is that I'm to observe my own reactions in everyday situations to increase my awareness. Oh, yes—most important—Kathy stressed that my observations will be most helpful if I use my Adult part for the task and ask my Critical Parent to be silent. The process is about noticing my behavior without harsh judgments. This allows change to take place more easily.

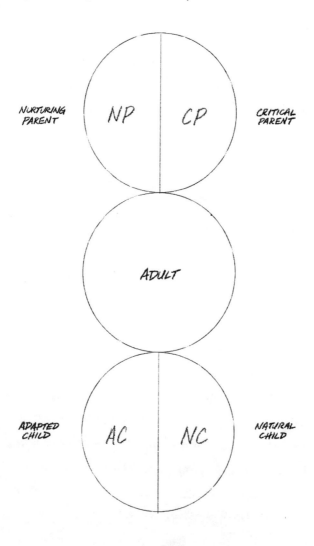

Pause Button

Tool #4 Observing Your Own Ego States (or your own snowperson, if you prefer!)

As with our other exercises, I suggest that you:

1. Select a quiet place and set aside ten to twenty minutes for yourself.
2. Draw three equal circles, one on top of the other
3. Draw a vertical line in the top circle so that it divides the circle in half. Label one half as Nurturing Parent and the other half as Critical Parent.
4. Label the middle circle Adult.
5. Divide the lowest circle in half with a vertical line. Label one half as Natural Child and the other half as Adapted Child.

Refer back to Erica's session with Kathy and diagram your own ego states. Also, look ahead to her cheat sheets, as they may help. You can find a drawing of the snowperson as described above in the appendix.

Here are some concepts about each part:

Parent Circle: This is your internal rule and guidebook.

When you were young, you heard and observed rules, customs, and grown-up interactions. Some of these made sense to you and you (literally) absorbed them. An example might be "Stop at a red light." Now you don't question what to do. When you see a red light, you know the rule.

Other times, you may have seen ineffective or dysfunctional patterns in your home or school. You may have told yourself, "I will never do that!" Perhaps you saw your mom submit to some abusive behavior. You told yourself, "If people are rude to you, you should speak up." You incorporated that rule into your internal Parent, and it may still be there today. Notice that the language of this part of the Parent is full of shoulds, shouldn'ts, musts, and oughts.

Regarding the Nurturing Parent, perhaps you were blessed with supportive parents. Since you benefited from their behaviors and values, you assimilated them into your own internal Parent. Today, you believe in those same child-rearing rules and techniques. Or, unfortunately, you may not have felt supported or nurtured, and so you created nurturing guidelines and behaviors very different to what you experienced as a child.

It is important for you to inventory the contents of your Parent parts. Much of the material was stored there long ago when you weren't as knowledgeable and experienced as you are today. You may find that some of it needs modifying or even discarding! Just doing the inventory typically produces insights and changes.

Adult Circle: This is your information processing center.

Your Adult part can be an astute observer searching for clues to who you are today and what you think, feel, and do in response to others. To access the Adult, take some slow breaths and listen to your internal dialogue. In other words, relax into your Adult. People who like the ego-state model find that from the vantage point of the Adult, they can listen to their other parts as they debate differing points of view. The Adult is an important ally for observing ourselves. We can ask the Adult to notice without judgment. This way, we are free to change behaviors that aren't working. We can get out of automatic responding. Just doing this often enhances a sense of power and can boost self-esteem.

Child Circle: Lots of fun and surprises may await you here.

Let's begin with the Natural Child, or as some call it, the Free Child. This is your uninhibited self. The ability to let go and have fun comes from here, as well as creativity and joy. It's not unusual for people to be out of touch with this part of themselves as they become responsible grown-ups, meeting goals and dreams and being very serious. Wouldn't it be an interesting world if grown-ups rushed outside at the first snowfall, as many children do, to catch snowflakes on their tongues? This is not intended to encourage adults to discard their goals and dreams, and we can't be childlike all the time. But learning how to access that natural self and let it be expressed adds spice to grown-up living and puts a spring (maybe even a hop) in one's step!

So, give some thought to your Natural Child. Write about the traits and personality style that you find there.

The second part of the Child—the Adapted Child—is also very important. Think of this part as the storehouse of your coping strategies, your responses to others. For example, "When Mom fussed at me, I ran and hid." Or, "When Mom fussed at me, I argued back and was loud." As a child, your ability to cope with authorities, rules, and values was limited because you were limited. You couldn't move out on your own. You weren't strong enough to meet some physical challenges. You couldn't get a job and/or drive a car.

So you had to create strategies to meet the daily challenges from peers, teachers, coaches, parents and grandparents, brothers and sisters, and so forth. The tactics that seemed to work got reinforced and absorbed into your Adapted Child. Obviously, some of them weren't that healthy (running away and hiding, for example). When you really examine your ego states, you will probably find many coping strategies that you will want to modify. Now, you are grown up. You have power, strength, and experience. You can create responses that will gain better results.

An important reminder: Use your Adult part as your guide when you are looking deeply into yourself. Just look for the facts. Try to avoid making judgments about anything you find. Put your Critical Parent on mute when you are looking at the other parts. You don't want to respond to criticism in this process by running and hiding from yourself. After all, almost everything can be changed. Your Nurturing Parent can help here too, supporting you on your quest for self-awareness with honesty.

These wonderful insights have been abbreviated and modified from the work of transactional analysts, as Erica told you in her August 20 blog. Additional texts on transactional analysis (usually referred to as TA) are listed in References.

September 27

I watched *Peter Pan* with my nieces and decided that my theme song should be, "I Won't Grow Up."

That's not totally true. I wouldn't go back to being a teenager for anything. I like the sense of being in control of my life, holding a job, building a future. But thinking again about the Adult in me that should be observing, adapting, and guiding my actions, I want to fold my arms and say, "No way, it's too much trouble. I'll stay just as I am, and you can't make me change."

Oh, right, the whole point of this exercise is that I want to change.

I've been searching for excuses to avoid looking at the sheet Kathy gave me and my homework—to focus on what she was trying to teach me. I was so desperate for a distraction that I agreed to go with my friend Loretta to an early morning race for one of the good causes she's always involved with. This one was Breast Cancer Research, and our assignment was to help out at the refreshment stand.

Five-thirty in the morning is dark—very dark. We got to our places in the refreshment tent and learned we were in charge of bananas, oranges, and protein bars.

For five hours I never saw a single face, just hands reaching out for one of the snacks. My job was to cut oranges into quarters and bananas into halves. Hundreds of them—quickly. Once the runners and walkers began to converge on us, I couldn't cut fast enough. More oranges. More bananas. More oranges. Still more bananas.

By 10:30 a.m., we had used up all of the fruit from the wall of boxes behind the tent. I smelled like day-old fruit salad—and I loved it—every tiring, smelly, juicy moment of it. When the amount of money raised was announced and a group of cancer survivors took the stage, I joined everyone in clapping wildly and crying a bit. I understood why Loretta gets involved in these volunteer activities. It's true: if you stop focusing on yourself and your own problems, life is a lot more fun.

My fingers are still puckered from the juice, but I have the confidence now to pull out Kathy's sheet and get back on track to a better understanding of myself.

Okay, here goes, straight from the cheat sheet:

Erica's Cheat Sheet

When I "Stop... Look... and... Listen"
With my awake ADULT, I can detach.

I can find out which part is in charge.
I can say, "Isn't that interesting that I (feel/
think/was behaving) that way?"

Note to self: Hey, you've started to do this. You're at least starting to observe your actions and reactions and find them interesting. Good job, Erica.

Back to Erica's Cheat Sheet:

Hints
Check out - how do I feel?
What words am I using?
How am I acting?
How are others reacting/acting toward me?

Results
I will have less stress because I can make
more sense of what is happening.
I can make wiser choices.
I can get along better with others.
I can have more fun!

I love these results. They're exactly what I was looking for.

There's more to the cheat sheet, but I'm tired. Will I dream of oranges and bananas while I sleep?

September 28

While I was still feeling so positive about the world and my place in it, I tackled the rest of the cheat sheet this morning. It requires a lot more attention. I have to think of each of the three circles of my snowperson, remember what they're about, and how they operate when they are (and therefore I am) working well.

Goals

Goals for the Adult:
To be empowered—to calmly keep the other parts out of trouble.
To reexamine all the materials to see what I want
to retain, and what I want to discard.
To get out of automatic so that new behaviors and
feelings can be created and strengthened.

Goals for the Parent:
To modify those rules that no longer make sense.
To use my nurturing skills to self-nurture.
To gently point out alternatives rather than criticize harshly.
To value thinking for myself, not blindly accepting
values and rules that might not work for me.

Goals for the Adapted Child:
To look again at my coping strategies and defenses.
To add new, empowered, grown-up strategies.

Well now, it's sure going to take a lot of practice to make these a part of my routine. I'm going to carry them around for a few days and pull them out now and again and hope they sink in.

For extra help, I'm also making a list of some of the various (positive and negative) feelings and thoughts typical of each part, to help me identify exactly who is in charge, and when!

The Child

> Freely expresses reactions
>
> May feel needy or helpless
>
> May feel hurt or guilty
>
> Creative
>
> Having fun
>
> Experiencing delight

The Parent

> Frowns of disapproval
>
> Nurturing
>
> Restrictions to keep me safe
>
> Use of "should" and "ought"

The Adult

> Isn't it interesting that something occurred?
>
> Not judging—just noticing
>
> Problem focused—not *who* is the problem,
>
> but *what* is the problem?
>
> Factual

September 29

A group of coworkers went out for drinks yesterday evening, and I tried out my new observant self.

Bobby, who must have been a court jester in a previous life, was his usual grating self. His style of humor is to pick out a victim and make that person the butt of his jokes. It's been my turn to be skewered on several occasions, and I could see that he was fixing on me as the evening's prey.

So okay, with my awake Adult, I can detach and observe how I am feeling in a situation. How do I feel at this point? Asocial, antisocial, annoyed - you get the gist. And why?

Bobby's remarks, pinning me like a frog in biology lab, made me feel dissected. I felt powerless, the way I always feel when my mother lists my faults and I get sarcastic to protect myself from the pain.

But I'm smarter now. I tried the strategy of the Adult. I took a nice deep breath and tapped into my ability to think logically. Immediately, I felt somehow empowered as I stayed calm and kept the vulnerable parts out of trouble. So I said to Bobby, "You are so witty; did you ever want to be a professional comedian?" Out came a torrent of stories about his childhood, his dreams, his need to settle for something practical instead of what he really wanted. Wait until I tell Kathy that she has created an amateur therapist. Really, I should have charged him for the session! I listened politely, feeling relieved that I was no longer his victim, and astonished that I had become his confidant instead.

I slipped out at the first opportunity, gloating all the way home that I followed one of the recommendations from my homework. If Bobby tries to tell me his life story again, I'm going to give him Kathy's card. I feel good, but I'm not even an expert at my own life yet. I certainly don't want to take on responsibility for the life of the court jester.

October 5

This romp through the land of snowmen seemed about all I could take, but there was Kathy sketching two snowpersons. The war of the snowpeople, I'm thinking?

Kathy asked me to think about what happens when Jack meets Jill. She suggested we picture Jill as someone who has rigid expectations of Jack (stored in her Critical Parent), believing that he'll always obey her rules, even if she doesn't tell him what they are. He will always be on time. He will always plan their dates and never deviate from what he has told her in advance. He will want to go where she wants to go, marry if she wants to marry, have children if she wants to have children.

According to Kathy, that could bring out the Adapted Child in Jack. The more expectations Jill puts on him, the more likely Jack is to resort to his coping strategies, stored from childhood, that produce freedom at any cost. If Jill expects him to be on time, he'll be late. If she dislikes spontaneity, he'll be Last-Minute Jack in planning things.

Jack and Jill will be hooked into painful misunderstandings unless they can get into their Adult parts and see the dynamics. Kathy says *hooked* is a term from transactional analysis, and she finds it to be a powerful metaphor. As I think about it, she is right (as usual). Hooks are sharp, and it hurts when they get stuck in you (I can speak from experience about this!). In this example, Jill's controlling Parent will only get more controlling, while Jack's free-spirited Child will get ever more willful and unpredictable. Calamity follows.

How do they salvage this relationship between two people who are at such cross-purposes? Kathy says this is where the insights they can gain from transactional analysis can be so helpful. This is at the heart of Dr. Berne's theory—understanding how ego states are involved in transactions between people. I take this to mean that they both need to get out of the Parent-Child dynamic and try relating from their Adult parts. The Adult in each of them could appreciate and respect the good aspects of the other's behavior and give a little. They could acknowledge their differences and strike a compromise.

They could reestablish their relationship so that they either don't get hooked by the other person, or they could decide that they're unwilling to compromise and let the relationship lapse without the angry recriminations that are so typical and so hurtful.

Whew, that's a lot to take in from just three circles.

Homework again. I need to come up with my own examples. I'm to look at relationships in my life when Parent and Child come into conflict, and Adult is apparently off in a corner somewhere. Kathy calls this a PAC scan (short for Parent-Adult-Child). I call it a painful reality check.

October 15

Rather than plunging into the maelstrom of a relationship that I've had with my mother or the disappointing relationships with men in my life, I decided to cut myself a little slack and try my new tools from TA to work on a less conflicted relationship. I picked one with a girlfriend, who is also a coworker. Come on, you can cut me some slack too! I'm trying!

This seems trivial as I write it, but it seemed positively monumental when it happened. Gretchen and I decided we would go to dinner and a movie on a Monday. It seemed a trifle decadent—going out on a school night. She's an excellent researcher, so she googled every movie in town and also every theater. Which one has the best sound quality? An upscale lobby? Stadium seating? As I said, she's quite the researcher.

We settled on a theater across town—not my preference, but I behaved from my Adult and reasoned that since Gretchen really wanted to go to this theater, and there was no reason not to except that I thought it was ridiculously out of the way (Critical Parent trying to speak up!), we would go.

First, though, there was dinner. I wanted a quick and inexpensive place because, after all, it was a Monday and this was a girls' outing, not a date. Gretchen, though, had researched a new ethnic restaurant—some fusion thing (yuck!). I got into my willful Child mode and refused to order anything except soup. It was called Mekong, and I swear they scooped it right out of an Asian river. I didn't even want to know what those things were that were floating in the broth.

I guess I showed her, right? Thanks to reverting to my willful Child, I had weird soup.

When we got to the theater, ready to see a light romantic comedy, Gretchen got all intrigued with a foreign film that was starting at the same time. I might have been interested, eager even, to change plans, except that the reason she even considered going to this movie (that she hadn't researched to death) was because the good-looking guy at the ticket counter said it was a great flick.

So I sat through the whole movie with Mekong soup gurgling in my stomach and bile creeping up my esophagus. It might have been a great movie. I don't know. I was too busy being mad. There's that Child again.

I can hear Kathy: "What could Erica have done if only she had accessed her Adult self?" Well, certainly ordered something better for dinner. I can see, looking at the situation from a distance, that I should have discussed with Gretchen my reluctance to see the foreign film, if in fact I was reluctant. To tell you the truth, I don't know if I was or not. I simply reacted in anger because she made a decision based on what I had decided were foolish grounds. Maybe she would have insisted on the foreign film. Maybe she would have listened to my reasoned argument that we knew nothing about it and we had been looking forward to the comedy. Then we might have gone to our original plan. Or we might even have separated so each of us got to see the movie of our choice and then gotten together after the movie to trade opinions.

How easy, rational, and fun that seems at a distance. In the midst of my internal drama (as well as the external one), I fell back on old patterns of wanting my way and not explaining how I felt. Instead, I went along with someone else's plans and then felt angry about it, blaming my friend because I didn't take control of my own happiness.

I think I've got a good sense of this Parent-Child-Adult relationship. It's slippery, though. I can see right now I'll have to practice it a lot before I get used to acting differently.

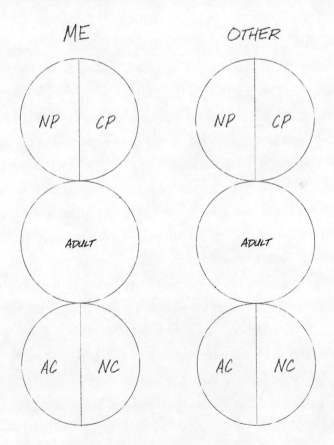

Pause Button

Tool #5 Create Your Own PAC Diagram

Again, in a quiet place, draw two sets of circles, (two snowpersons as Erica calls them) for this Parent-Adult-Child Diagram.

Label the top circle of each Nurturing Parent (NP) and Critical Parent (CP); Adult (A) in the middle circle of each; and Adapted Child (AC) and Natural Child (NC) in both bottom circles.

Please refer back to Kathy's discussion of Jack and Jill. If you were constructing them, you would show lots of rules and expectations in Jill's CP. You might draw a diagonal line from Jill's CP down to Jack's AC, where he has stored his responses (created in childhood and still a real part of him). Jack gets hooked by Jill's criticisms and responds to her in ways that are automatic and ineffective in resolving their problems. We want to avoid such interactions in our own lives, and yet we find ourselves hooking others and being hooked by them.

The first step in unlocking these powerful (and often painful) dynamics is for us to do a thorough inventory of our own ego states (our own selves or snowpersons) as you did in Tool #4.

For Tool #5, continue that careful analysis by picturing a conflict in which you were one of the participants. Label one of the sets of circles (one of the snowpersons) "Myself" or "Me." Put the name of the other person over the second set of circles. Recall what occurred, especially what was said, as well as any significant nonverbal communication.

Step back and observe this diagram and, with your Adult super-sleuth, describe the action.

If we asked Erica for an example, she might say, "I think that Tony, a guy from my office, is an example of someone coming from his Critical Parent. He is often very rigid about office policies. When he speaks, his voice is loud, and he wiggles his finger at people. I think my Adapted Child gets hooked. I have always gotten embarrassed when people speak to me loudly. I often think the other person is a bully, and I get angry. I really get hooked by rigidity too. So then I avoid him and make wisecracks behind his back, seeing him as a villain. Now I see that I can make a different choice: take a deep breath and get to my Adult, so I can hear that he is alarmed about an office situation and maybe even a little anxious. I can ask questions to clarify. I don't have to make him into a bad guy, or take on the role of victim."

Looking at these dynamics in this way, may feel strange at first. People who like this tool say, however, that it soon becomes part of them, and they can picture the dynamics easily and quickly. They incorporate the ego-state diagram so well that they begin to think, feel, and act in new and more effective ways with others. They really do change. And so can you.

October 20

I took my newfound wisdom for a trial run with mixed results.

My boss gave me an assignment that I thought was a silly use of my time. Immediately, I could feel the instinct to revert to Child and either make a fuss or do it with resentment. A triumph, though: I stopped myself, thought of how Erica acting from her Adult would approach this, and it worked! I agreed to do the assignment and added that I had a suggestion about how we might accomplish it. I could see the astonishment on his face and then the smile as he acknowledged that yes, my suggestion was actually a better approach and we would try it my way.

So please put points in the Adult Erica column. If I can keep this up, I can see that a promotion may be possible after all.

Never get cocky. I was so proud of myself for that one that I didn't see this next one coming.

My sister invited me to go shopping with her—just the two of us. Her husband offered to watch the kids while we had a day out, complete with lunch. Food, no problem. Shopping? There was that Child again. I picked up a shirt that was a bit wild for my tastes, but interesting. Laura looked at the label, noted that it was dry-clean only, and remarked that I was not good at remembering to get things to the cleaners. I slid right into old habits. I heard her speaking right out of her Critical Parent, and whether she was right or not, I was so angry!

Actually, her judgment is on target. My philosophy is that if a piece of clothing can't withstand the washing machine, it doesn't belong in my closet, except for a few good suits that I wear to work. Remembering to take them to the dry cleaners is only slightly easier than remembering to pick them up again.

Okay, so she was right. Did that stop me? No—I had to act like a petulant child, telling her something along the lines of "you're not the boss of me," and buy the shirt.

Expect to see this shirt used as a cleaning rag within the next two weeks. I should not have bought it. My sister was right. I was reacting automatically from my Adapted Child. Oh, where were you, my Adult, when I needed you? Your rational voice got drowned out by my petulant child! And by the way, I don't even like the shirt.

Kathy will love this story. More work to do.

November 9

My high school physics teacher would tell you that my passing grade was an act of mercy on her part. There is one principle of physics, though, that I am sure about. If you beat your head (my head, in this case) against a brick wall, your head (my head) will get badly damaged and the wall won't show a mark.

That's how I was feeling before my next session with Kathy. No matter how hard I try, I don't seem to be breaking through the obstacles in my approaches to people. I keep making the same mistakes, even though I know the words to use and the concepts behind them. Well, not enough to pass a test, but I know them better than I ever learned physics. I've got all these insights, and they just depress me.

Kathy was her usual patient, optimistic, nurturing self. First, she insisted that I think about the things I've done right. It seems so simple to start with the positive. I remember someone telling me once that we talk about starting out on the right foot. What is the opposite of that? Not the wrong foot, just the left foot. But I immediately start with the wrong things I've done instead of the right.

I'll bet if I could master that little maneuver—start with the right things—I'd move along much better.

Anyway, Kathy was not willing to let me wallow in pity or negativity. She went right back to those Parent-Adult-Child parts that she's been teaching me.

"You've gotten yourself into the Critical Parent mode," she told me. "You're judging yourself the way you recall your mother judging you. Remember what happens when your Critical Parent takes control. For you, there is an immediate move to your Adapted Child, who gets very resentful."

Oh, yes indeed, I know that. So how do I stop it, other than running to her every time I need a Nurturing Parent fix?

Kathy reminded me again about the power of noticing. She wants me to notice, not judge. And then she did the most wonderful thing. She asked that I close my eyes, breathe deeply, and just listen as she guided me through a beautiful meditation. Kathy said she had planned it for one of our upcoming sessions. Meditating is one of the important tools in the tool box, but we hadn't gotten to it yet. She decided not to wait—that I needed one right away.

She told me that being really present to yourself takes practice, but that the skill is well worth developing. As always, I felt immensely better after the session. The meditation exercise was wonderful, and I am committed to getting better at this process of noticing without judging.

Pause Button

Tool #6 Meditation

You may enjoy reading this meditation, but if you would like to listen instead (or do both), go to the website (www.kendrabrownphd.com) for free audio downloads. This one is #1 *Snowflakes*. Caution: Do not listen to this meditation when you are driving or operating equipment—even cooking dinner! Find a quiet place and sit for a few minutes. When you are through listening, allow yourself a few minutes to re-enter your regular world, fully awake.

Kathy's meditation:

> Imagine that you're a guest at a mountain lodge. You notice, with pleasure, the room in which you are sitting. The furniture and the colors are soothing and comfortable. It's as if this place were designed just for you. You feel secure and nurtured. You may hear the crackling of a fire in the fireplace or be aware of pleasant smells. The sights, the sounds, the smells—all of these things add to your sense of peace and calm.
>
> You have an amazing view through the large window beside you. Outside, you observe a soft, gray winter sky and watch as some giant snowflakes drift past. If you were outside, you might try to catch them in your hands and examine their patterns before

they melted away. Each snowflake is wondrous. Each snowflake is different. One snowflake is no better or worse than another.

But you are warm, snuggled inside, with no need to analyze or evaluate them. You are content to watch through your window as the snowflakes continue to fall gently outside.

It may occur to you, as you sit peacefully, that these snowflakes are like the thoughts and feelings that cross the window of your mind. It's been said that simply noticing them in mindful meditation can be very healing and helpful. Just letting each one come and go, with no analysis, no evaluation. Just noticing and letting go.

Then, off in the distance, you see a hiker. She looks as if she's in a hurry, perhaps trying to get to the lodge ahead of the snowfall. As she walks down the trail, she dislodges a small rock, not much bigger than a pebble. You may find yourself fascinated by this rock's downward journey, noticing that as it rolls over and over, it becomes a snowball, gathering the snow into itself and becoming bigger. It gathers debris too, small sticks and gravel as it rolls downward. You're not alarmed. It's headed away from the lodge and soon plummets to the bottom. You watch as the snow and debris it accumulated are scattered around.

It may occur to you that anything or anyone in the snowball's path would have been affected by it, could even have become part of it.

It may occur to you: How similar this is to times when I get balled up in my thoughts and feelings and become part of a drama I've created in my mind. And then the drama takes over, just like the snowball rolling out of my control. Only afterward do I realize what happened and how I came to be in a heap of debris.

And then you may feel pleased to notice that, from your window, you have not been swept away into a snowball. Instead, you have watched the snow come and go. You have remained safe, quiet, and calm.

Wouldn't it be wonderful to sit beside your mind's window and observe thoughts and feelings with no attempt to catch them, analyze them, or evaluate them? To simply notice them? How comfortable you could be in your window seat, apart from the snow and the snowball, and not a part of it!

And you could even add: There's a wonderful bonus to this experience. I can repeat it for myself daily. If I choose to, I can find a comfortable place to sit, away from any distractions. I can picture the lodge, or some other lovely spot. I can watch and observe as my thoughts and feelings come across my mind's window. I don't judge them or try to grab them for analysis. I just let them come and go as I notice them.

Doing this provides my body and mind with a special space, a small time of peace and ease and relaxation. And in this space, I may gain a clearer picture of who I am, what I am thinking about, and how I am feeling. Practicing this enables me to live more peacefully and effectively. It is a gift I give myself. When it is time to return to regular daily activity, I can gently stir my body awake and return to full consciousness and awareness.

November 12

I've been thinking back on those dreadful relationships I've had with guys over the past decade, and I gave myself a gold star. How do I rate a gold star? Certainly not because of my behavior. No, it's because I think I finally understand a bit about what went wrong.

My first inclination, as you know, is to look at everything from my Critical Parent seat of judgment and blame myself. Then, I quickly blame others as a defense mechanism. Next, of course, come the sarcastic remarks.

All of this pie-making and snowperson constructing has helped me view my past more intelligently and objectively. I see now that I was too quick to assign blame, either to myself or to others, instead of just noticing and observing what was going on and choosing to act from my Adult.

Take Roscoe, for example. Oh please, I was ready for anyone to take Roscoe! Except that it hurt me when we broke up. Even a wretch like Roscoe seemed preferable to nobody.

I blamed him because he wanted to spend every weekend immersed in sports, either playing sports with his friends or watching sports with them. Meanwhile, I sulked because I wanted to do things with him, just him and me.

So who's to blame? No one. I startle myself that I'm able to write that. Roscoe was just being Roscoe. But I wanted him to be someone else. Instead of enjoying things I like to do with my own friends, I allowed myself to feel dependent on Roscoe, wanting him to abandon his friends and his ways of enjoying himself. No wonder we argued all the time. I'm just lucky that he walked out when he did. I might have clung to him, making both of us miserable, until we had done some real damage, like getting married in the hopes of making it all better. People have done things like that—and it could have been me.

Now I would color in my Roscoe pie with lots of yellow to show that I contributed to the problem at least as much as he did. But mostly I would put in another color—maybe white for open space—to show that – even though Roscoe and I are generally okay people (I'm OK/You're OK) - we simply didn't belong together.

I hope I get smart enough on all of this to make a relationship work before I'm too decrepit to care.

How's this for a great idea? When I meet a guy in the future, I'll do a PAC scan on him. I'll try to figure out how his Parent-Adult-Child ego states are working and whether we're meeting each other from compatible states, or the ingredients we're bringing to the relationship will just end up in a really messy pie.

November 15

Since I was a teen, I've been taking those silly personality tests that you find in magazines and online. Do I like orange better than green? Then I'm destined for an exciting future. Do I sing in the shower, but not in my car? Then I'm inhibited, though not always. Do I remember to carry lip gloss at all times, even if I forget my wallet? Of course I never forget my lip gloss!

When I moaned to Kathy about Roscoe and how I keep making the same mistakes over and over again, she suggested that I try a more scientific personality analysis than the ones I'm used to. She sent me to the Internet to find the Myers-Briggs Type Indicator.

I took the assessment online, and I want you to know that you are looking at an extrovert who loves spontaneity. I already knew I was outgoing, but the in-depth information was so helpful and somehow affirming.

So what difference does this make? Is it more useful than knowing that when I see the letter B, I see blue, or that I eat my vegetables all at once instead of spread out with the rest of the meal?

Kathy took me on a quick tour of what the Myers-Briggs says about me and how the information it provides not only helps me understand myself better—it also gives me insights about why some relationships flow easily and others require lots of effort. No wonder it's so easy to be with people who share my same personality preferences—not that I'd want that all of the time. It could be very boring.

Because I love spontaneity, I need to be aware that someone who insists on knowing exactly how long it will take to get to the movies, even down to the amount of time that may be spent waiting for red lights, is not someone I can relate to. We would frustrate each other terribly.

I wondered if knowing that I'm an extrovert would mean I'll always want to be with people just like me? Sounds as though this could lead to spontaneous combustion—everyone talking, everyone engaging, and no one listening. It would be like a constant mash-up.

Kathy's guidance was helpful once again. What you learn from Myers-Briggs, she said, helps as you encounter others and analyze why you seem to fit together or not. It takes away the idea of "You're not OK" or "I'm not OK." We simply are who we are.

She suggested that extroverts often bring out the best in introverts, and vice versa, as long as each is prepared to respect the other's orientation toward life and events. I have friends like Lisa, who loves to listen more than to talk and who is ready to be spontaneous—provided someone else says, "Let's go." So we do great together. On the other hand, one of the many guys I've dated was an introvert, and I remember how my ideas for fun activities made him really twitchy. So, another tool for the tool box: the Myers-Briggs assessment.

Pause Button

Tool #7 Taking the Myers-Briggs

The Myers-Briggs Type Indicator (MBTI) is a personality inventory. You can take it from a licensed professional who has been certified by MBTI (usually a person like Kathy), or you can take it online (www. MBTIComplete.com).

This site—like a professional—provides the assessment, the results, and the interpretation. I think you will find the material it provides to be very straightforward and self-explanatory. However, you may want to learn more about the material, and a licensed professional who knows the indicators may provide additional information for you.

It is a highly useful test, in my opinion. It is not designed to assess mental health issues. It simply provides useful—and often fun—information about personality preferences, yours or others, and how they differ.

The Myers-Briggs is based on the work of Dr. C. G. Jung and his personality types. Two of the types Dr. Jung observed, for example, are extroversion and introversion. An *extrovert* is a person who gets energy from social contact. If an extrovert is by him- or herself for a long time, he or she will typically feel unhappy or drained in various ways. An *introvert*, on the other hand, is a person who gets energy from within. An introvert would typically not enjoy a weekend of back-to-back parties with no time or space to get away by him- or herself. Dr. Jung did not classify either extroverts or introverts as better or worse—just different.

When we see differences between ourselves and others, we often interpret these in negative ways. (He just doesn't want us to go to the party. He knows I like parties. He doesn't care enough about me to go!) When we learn about types, we can see that differences are just differences, and we can work around them or choose friends, especially intimate ones, who are closer in type to ourselves. Many self-help books have been written about using the results of the Myers-Briggs indicator to improve both personal and professional happiness. I have listed some of these books in our appendix.

November 25

So, you might want to ask, how are things with your mother?

Family dinners look so great in holiday ads, with everyone dressed nicely, seated around a beautifully decorated table, sharing heartwarming stories. My version of them is more like a scene where outright hysteria could break out at any moment.

We gathered last week at my sister's house to celebrate the birthday of my brother-in-law, Drew. I'm very fond of him. He's a genuinely nice guy, and he has a skill that we all value enormously: he can turn the conversation away from topics that get my mother, sister, and me embroiled in brutal verbal warfare.

Kathy told me this would be a great opportunity to watch my own behavior and the behaviors around me, so I decided to approach the dinner with a certain amount of curiosity rather than my usual dread. What ego states did I observe myself coming from? And where did I see others coming from? That means (in case you're not paying close enough attention, Dear Reader) that I planned to be in my Adult state, observing and not judging or reacting.

Watching the dinner as though it were a play, I was surprised to see immediately that my sister and mother were not the unified force I had always imagined them to be. My mother was critical of how my sister was interacting with her children—typical grandmotherly stuff, I guess. Mom seemed willing to let the kids do pretty much what they wanted; at the same time, she was criticizing my sister for the way Laura was correcting them. It seemed to me that Mom was acting as though she were the boss in the house. Quite a different approach to discipline than she used when we were little and she *really* was the boss of the house.

What really amazed me was watching my sister deal with it. She stayed calm, repeated her words to the children, and then suggested that they take Grandma into the family room and show her their artwork from school. Good strategy! She seemed to accept that Mom's controlling was coming from her Critical Parent, and she simply shifted direction. My sister acted just like an adult who stays balanced and was actually in control.

Thanks to the kids having stories to tell, with prompts from Drew, the dinner itself went well. We all got into the spirit of the stories and played along, remembering bits of songs that seemed to fit, and Mom even tried out a few voices from old cartoon characters. Kathy would say, I think, that we were in our Natural Child states and having fun because there was no Critical Parent on the scene.

Once the kids left the table, though, we moved away from the fun. Danger, danger! Don't go to the Adapted Child part, I kept telling myself, the part where you feel like you need to rebel. Think about hanging out in your Adult part

Well, I can think about staying in my Adult part, but my mouth seems permanently linked to a petulant Child. I'd say it took about four minutes before my mother said something that I took to be a criticism. Off I went, ranting and raving about living my life on my own terms, blah, blah, blah. Drew, bless him, interrupted and asked about a movie he knew I had seen. Ah, redirection. I'm seeing this as a really good technique to bring people back to a place where they can interact more effectively.

Observing Laura from my theater seat, I was amazed at what I was learning about her. I never noticed the techniques she developed over the years to interact successfully with our mother. She frequently asked Mom for advice, which I knew she had no intention of taking, but it made my mother feel good and brought out a gentle quality in her. If I get advice, I feel compelled to respond exactly how I feel, which is usually annoyed that someone is telling me what to do.

Another of her strategies that fascinated me was her selective hearing. Maybe having children teaches you that. I was intrigued to see how well it works with adults. My sister could hear my mother making what seemed to me to be outrageously irritating comments about the house, about how to clean up after dinner, about what the children should or should not be doing in their spare time. Laura seemed not to hear. She didn't react. No wonder Mom loves her best!

On the whole, while I wasn't proud of my behavior at the dinner table, I also wasn't as horrified as usual. I can't say that it's because the lessons I've learned from Kathy have become an automatic part of me yet or that I'm easily behaving from a completely changed internal operating system. Definitely, though, the technique of observing others is a valuable one and a good first step. I'm grateful to transactional analysis that I'm starting to see how Mom's Critical Parent is only a problem if one of us acts like a Child. If no one acts that way, then the moment passes and we all get along.

December 2

Chicago, here I come!

Apparently my new tools are working on the job, if not so much on the home front. I've taken to heart Kathy's advice about observing both my own behavior and that of others. Now I can see that sometimes the people around me are acting out of fear, which makes them strike out at someone or something before anything can strike them. Other times, people seem to be acting from those old models that still trip me up—for example, reacting to authority as though it's a battle between Critical Parents and Adapted Children instead of reasonably setting up rules from their Adult ego states that could help their company operate effectively.

So I've made a conscious effort to act from my Adult at work. At thirty-one, I really can't claim that this is any great accomplishment! On the other hand, you know me, and it is a great accomplishment.

Kathy assures me that as I transform myself, I'll get better and better at choosing the place from which I want to act. I can act from my Child with Gabby if that's my choice, and I can be successful at work acting from my Adult. Again, it's my choice.

Anyway, my new and improved behavior seems to be paying off because I've been chosen for the management training I've been longing for. I'll be spending three weeks in Chicago as part of a very small team from the company. We'll attend seminars together, get individual leadership training, and develop a whole new division of the company.

Get this: When my boss told me I'd been selected for the program, he complimented me on my "maturity" and my ability to form "productive relationships" with my coworkers. Who? Me?

I called Kathy immediately. This is her triumph as well as mine, although she of course graciously insisted that the credit was all mine.

When I think about how others are acting and how I, in turn, am responding, I amaze myself. Really! This mindful attention that Kathy talked about is powerful stuff.

December 15

I should call this piece "Meditations on They."

Kathy would probably describe it more appropriately as another reflection on "I'm OK/ They're Not OK."

Since Kathy helped me tune in to what is happening around me, I've been noticing how many times we blame "them" for whatever is wrong. "They" are making a mess of the country. "They" are wasting our tax dollars. "They" can't get the traffic signals right.

We're always assigning blame to some vague group of people. I remember that my dad used to do this all the time. It was as though there was a conspiracy against him and everything he tried to accomplish. "They" were always goofing up his best efforts.

Today I found myself doing the same thing. I started judging the "theys" who operate the grocery store, the coffee shop, the cleaners, you name it. They are as personable as shredded wheat, as sharp as a door knob, as competent as an oyster shell! You know I could go on from there. But I stopped myself finally and remembered Kathy's pies. How much of the irritation that I was feeling had to do with "them" and how much was me? Suddenly, I started seeing a lot of yellow swirling through the pies I was envisioning.

"They" may be adding to traffic, mismanaging agencies, and so on. But "they" are not making a mess of my life. "They" aren't really in control of my peace of mind, unless I allow them to be.

Don't I just feel smug! I think I've learned something important.

Next time I see Kathy, I'm going to try out my Theory of They on her. She might want to add it to her pie recipe.

March 6

Where have I been?

How I wish at this point, dear blog, I could steal a line from Jane Austen and write, "Dear Reader, I married him."

Nope, that's not the story. Certainly not the ending of the story, anyway.

I stopped writing because I felt that I had achieved all that I had wanted: An interesting job, thanks to the training and promotion I got; a sort of truce in my relationship with my family, even with my mother (but that's partly because of this next thing I'm going to list); and a great guy in my life.

His name was Ted. Well, his name is still Ted, but he's more like Mud to me. I met him around the holidays, always a magical time. We were introduced by friends. Isn't that just the best way? I wouldn't have minded if we had met by accident or on the Internet, but we met at a restaurant where mutual friends were having a going-away party before they left for new adventures on the other side of the world.

Because it happened so casually, I didn't have a chance to sabotage myself. We just started talking and found lots in common, laughed a lot, and felt like friends. There wasn't that icky, sticky stuff at the beginning where you're flirting just to find out whether the guy is worth the effort. This was effortless.

We started dating. I was so proud and happy to introduce him to my family and take him to a company party. Everyone liked him immediately, even Mom. He has a stable job (that won him lots of points with her), lots of interests (that won him lots of points with me), and good sense of humor (that will win points anywhere).

I was totally in love. I stopped seeing friends and built my weekly schedule around moments when Ted and I could be together. We talked about moving in together. I could feel a nesting sensation coming on. How would our tastes blend into furnishings for our first apartment?

Whatever he wanted to do, I wanted to do. Until what he wanted to do was to be free of me.

Aaaccchhh! How did that happen?

Now I'm reluctant to tell people that my dream guy is just a fading memory, one that still feels very fresh to me. How did I screw this up?

I'm looking through my tool kit that Kathy helped me create. And I think that I may need to go in for a major tune-up.

March 16

It only took a sentence and a smile from Kathy for me to realize how much I had missed her. She makes me feel safe—and maybe not as stupid as I sometimes feel out on my own.

But I know her by now, and so I was prepared for her to push and prod me to use my tool kit. I wanted sympathy from her, a few words about how cruel Ted had been to desert me, poor me. Well, that never happened. And I knew it wouldn't. There's no hammer in the tool kit to smash a reality I don't like, there's no eraser to rub them out, and there are no tissues for crying in the corner. Kathy asked me to access my Adult ego state and examine my relationship with Ted and what may have turned my Cinderella-like coach into a splattered pumpkin.

Okay, here goes: I loved the moments when Ted and I were having fun, feeling free and easy with each other, both of us feeling okay. Kathy said it sure sounded like we were in that wonderful position of "I'm OK/You're OK" and that we were enjoying being free kids together. I agreed. That's exactly where I was with Ted.

We were both okay when we related as Adults too. How could I not think that he was my whole world, where everything was and always would be perfect?

Oh, I see! I got stuck in some childlike wishful thinking. I wanted to believe that happily ever after could be my new state of being.

And Kathy helped me see that the more I clung to my insistence that everything was perfect and had to stay that way, the more I was coming from my Critical Parent ego state. I made Ted my whole world, and I was insisting that he behave in my world exactly the way I designed it. Why couldn't he just be perfect? Why did he have to be late sometimes? How could he let work get in the way of our plans? Why did he have to have a night out with the guys when I didn't feel any need for a night out with the girls? In the past, I would have solved my dilemma by labeling Ted as "Not OK." But oh, he's more than okay. So I must be the one who's creating the problem.

Right now you're filling in the details, aren't you? You know that I started to feel very vulnerable, and that always leads to sarcasm, and that never leads anywhere good. He kept on behaving from his Adult ego state, and I slipped into my rebellious Child ego state, and then it was over.

At this point, Kathy took me in a direction I hadn't expected. She started talking about villages. I pictured those scenes that people create under Christmas trees, where the lights come on in the little cottages and puffs of smoke come from chimneys. Or maybe the quaint villages of a British murder mystery, where right after tea, the most horrible crimes occur.

My fantasies aside, what Kathy had in mind was for me to think of a life—my life—as a part of a village. "We need lots of people, different people, in our lives," Kathy told me, "for us to be mentally healthy. Think about all the people you interact with and how each of them brings out a facet of your personality. You have slightly different interactions with each of them. You're not a one-dimensional person. No one is. You need many people to form your village—your support system."

She helped me understand that I had closed out everyone else in my village and had depended solely on Ted for all of my emotional needs. No wonder he ran for the hills. I can see that it's an awful burden to carry for someone. But I loved him so much. I really thought he was all I needed.

"No one can be everything you need," Kathy said as directly as she's ever said anything to me. She also explained that we all need and depend on others. That is healthy. What isn't healthy is to place all your dependency needs on just a few people, or even worse, on one person. By creating a village, we spread our dependency needs out.

So if I'm building a village that holds everything I need, what do I need? A twenty-four-hour coffee shop with wireless Internet, an on-call hair stylist, a market with a sumptuous prepared-foods bar!

Okay, seriously, Kathy helped me to understand that everyone needs a variety of people, not just one or two, for a healthy life. For me, that means family. It means people at work. It means friends who like to travel. It means friends who like to meet and talk. It means organizations where I can feel useful. I even picture a bit of vacant land in my village where someone or something new could move in.

By putting all of the responsibility for my life and happiness on Ted, I hurt myself. I cut off my friends and my interests, and that made me feel so vulnerable that I fell back into bad patterns of behavior. I cut off the possibilities of new and interesting things and people, and I turned away from the people who were already in my village who had meant so much to me.

Just as I was about to throw myself into the "I am stupid" mode that I do so well, Kathy yanked me back. After all, I didn't destroy the village that I had built over the years; I just ignored it. The village was still there. I could go back and rebuild those relationships I had neglected. Kathy reminded me that I could build out my village even more by being open to new relationships and by actively seeking out the people and activities that could make my life richer.

It was a great session. I thought that I needed someone to tell me that I had been badly treated. Kathy's insistence that I use the tool kit to figure out what went wrong was so helpful. And I left not feeling "poor me" at all. I have calls to make to people I like, and I have places to go where I know they'll still remember me. Plus, I think I should look into volunteer work. I really liked being behind the scenes of that race a few months back.

I'm building my village.

April 30

Don't even talk to me about parents who over schedule their kids: soccer, hockey, tennis, dance, gymnastics, reading tutors, and maybe even advanced calculus for the little geniuses. I just did the same thing to myself.

I got so into the village idea that Kathy suggested that I'm the victim of urban blight. I kept adding intriguing little cottages until today I found myself ready to demolish entire neighborhoods.

I signed up for a few classes at the local community college. Who doesn't want to know how to make exquisite cupcakes and speak Mandarin? Then I found a group of professional women who meet for lunch every other week and talk about business and careers. It's really a great group, and I'm glad to be a part of it. But then I also added a book club, a gym membership (turns out you actually have to exercise, in addition to paying the membership fee, for any good to come of it), and a foreign movie discussion group that watches the most depressing movies I could ever imagine.

Good result: I haven't had time to feel too bad about Ted. Bad result: All I want to do is curl up on my couch and mindlessly scroll through Facebook. Even worse, I heard myself wishing for a Ted replacement: A solve-it-all perfect prince so that I wouldn't have to do all this work! I know that isn't the solution.

Just this week, I see I've scheduled something for every single evening, along with a few lunch appointments. Shouldn't I be happy? Mostly, I'm tired. And when my sister called to invite me to a family dinner, I almost cried. No, my calendar cannot handle one more social event!

Obviously I'm doing something wrong here. I'm tempted to whip up a batch of red velvet cupcakes, do the swirly stuff I learned in class last week, and stuff myself silly.

It's time for a Kathy fix.

Pause Button

Tool #8 Building Your Village

The goal of building your village is to become interdependent. As Kathy told Erica, we are dependent on others. Think of the most successful, happy men and women you know. They have people in their lives on whom they depend. People who have built successful careers have mentors, employees, important contacts, and so on. Healthy adults have a network of friends—people they've met in business, social gatherings, volunteer work, clubs, church, and so forth.

As a psychologist, I've worked with many patients who suffer depression at least partly due to isolation. These people have moved away from their homes and neighborhoods, clubs and churches to sunny Florida, where they planned to celebrate and enjoy their golden years. Only they failed to realize they had left their support systems behind. Those systems took time to build, and once they were in place, it was easy to take them for granted and not really count them as blessings until they were left behind.

I've also worked with many people who are angry and resentful because their spouses or significant others have "let them down." Without realizing it, they grew to depend solely on one person for their entertainment, encouragement, and enlightenment. Imagine! Yet, it happens all of the time. Perhaps it is a kind of wishful (magical) thinking—the prince or princess who makes all their dreams come true.

And finally, there are people like Erica, who haven't found the prince yet, but are searching earnestly and even desperately. And we have already seen what happens when she tried to give Ted that job. His response was to get on his white horse and head for the hills!

Building a village—a network of support—can actually be fun. Once constructed, you may notice that you feel much more secure. There's bound to be someone available to go to that movie if you have a list of possible candidates, rather than counting on just one overtaxed prince! You may also experience a sense of freedom and empowerment. When your support comes from several sources, you may be less willing to accept poor behavior from others. This results in feeling better about yourself and stronger.

Picture yourself in a boat that has lost power. There are oars and you can see the shore, although it will take some work to get there and it is beginning to rain. If there is only one other person in the boat with you, and that person refuses to row, complains about the weather, and only rows half-heartedly, you are not in a good spot. On the other hand, if your boat contains several people with multiple oars, even if the complaining person is in the boat, you're soon going to be on shore, safe and dry.

To carry out the village theme: When you select the various huts (those places that will provide some support, some entertainment, and so on), I encourage you to think of what you like to do and look into activities, volunteer positions, or clubs where you can easily meet with others who like to do the same things. For example, if you like to hike, you could join a hiking club. If you like to sing, look around for a community choir. I encourage starting with organized groups first because if you try to build your village solely with individuals, it takes longer. As many people have learned, it takes time to build really strong friendships.

Finally, in order to say yes to membership in clubs or work in volunteer positions, you will also need to be able to say no if the activity just isn't right for you. Read ahead to Erica's next session and the meditation that follows in Tool #9. Hopefully, this will be helpful to you.

May 10

She laughed, of course. Kathy finds my predicaments very amusing, and I must admit that I also had to laugh as I explained how a girl with nothing much to do now wants to hire a scheduling assistant.

I wrote this down exactly as she said it, and I'm going to have it tattooed on some body part: "You learned to say yes. That's good. Now it's time to also learn to say no."

Kathy said it was time for another of her favorite meditations. She asked me to make myself comfortable, take some nice deep breaths, and close my eyes. I loved this meditation, so Kathy gave me a written copy, and I'm including the whole thing here in my blog. She said it is patterned after one she loves from Virginia Satir.

Pause Button

Tool #9 The Golden Medallion

As with all relaxation, self-hypnosis, or meditation exercises, you should only do them when you are in a quiet place, away from competing activities, and not operating any kind of machinery. After these exercises, give yourself a few minutes to gently become fully awake and conscious.

The Golden Medallion

I'd like for you to imagine that you've been given a free visit to a wonderful spa. As you look around this special place, you realize that it is peaceful, serene, and safe. You may enjoy taking a few minutes to look around and notice the beauty of this place. You might walk around the gardens, which are full of flowers. Perhaps there is a water fountain, and you stop beside it to listen to the pleasant sounds of the flow. Everything about this place is just right, as if it were created for you: the sights, the sounds, even the pleasant smells.

As you continue your walk, you may find, to your delight, a place to rest and recline. What a gift—to be nurtured in so many ways. You may want to take a few minutes to just soak up all of these treats.

After a while, a kind-looking woman approaches. She says she has yet another gift for you: a small golden medallion. She asks you to read what is engraved on each side. On one side of the medallion, the word *yes* has been engraved. There are some sparkly bits, like tiny jewels, around the edge. She asks you what you think of this side. "Oh," you might reply, "I am familiar with yes. It's pretty easy to say yes." The kind lady just smiles and asks that you turn the medallion over and read the other side.

When you do, you may be surprised to see the word *no* engraved in a beautiful script and see that it also has lovely tiny jewels. The kind lady waits for your response. Perhaps you will tell her that you hadn't realized that no could be just right too. The lady smiles again and says she hopes you will remember that no is just as good as yes and that you may choose to respond using either side. What is most important is that you choose the answer that is best for you. Unlike flipping a coin, allowing your decisions to be made for you, or leaving them to chance (as in "heads I go and tails I stay"), you may flip the medallion to the side that works best for you. You can say yes to people, places, and things that work for you. You can say no to those that don't. You can even thank people for asking—and still say no.

You may want to take a few more minutes to really soak up all the restful, calming feelings of your special spa. Of course, even the most wonderful vacations come to an end, and when it is just the right time, you may choose to come back to your normal state of wakefulness and full consciousness—moving around gently in your chair and then opening your eyes—fully awake and alert. You can bring the image of your jeweled medallion with you as a reminder that both yes and no are attractive options.

(Adapted from *Meditations and Inspirations* by Virginia Satir)

Note: You may enjoy listening to the Golden Medallion on our website: www.kendrabrownphd.com

Cupcakes, movies, even Mandarin! I said yes to everything

because I was so intent on finding friends and interests. I let quantity overtake quality in my life. Seriously, I think I was so scared that people wouldn't want me that I grabbed at everything that went by. And if I apply this to my relationships with men, I see the parallel. I'm so scared not to be wanted that I say yes to things that a saner, more confident Erica would say no to immediately. My medallion has been stuck on the yes side, and I didn't realize the beauty of the reverse!

By taking a few minutes to listen to the medallion meditation, I feel more confident about saying "no, thanks" to some of the activities I frantically annexed into my village.

Why do I get so scared? Kathy assured me that when you're making changes, you can easily become anxious and fall away from the place where "I'm OK/You're OK." The important thing is to have tools that help you to control the anxiety and give yourself the space you need to reestablish your equilibrium.

"That's why meditation and relaxation exercises are such valuable tools," she told me. And I could see that these were the real jewels I was getting from her. They can help me use all the other new tools I've been learning. I love the Golden Medallion meditation, and Kathy gave me two more—very different—that I'm also copying into my blog. They don't take much time, but Kathy says that putting them into my weekly schedule will really pay off.

Pause Button

Tool #10 Progressive Muscle Relaxation

This is a well-researched technique developed by American physician Edmund Jacobson in the 1920s. It involves alternately tensing and relaxing various muscle groups throughout the body. Dr. Jacobson noted that when we are anxious, we tense our muscles. He proposed that we reverse the process by countering this tension with relaxation. Thus, we provide the brain with a message that we are not anxious. In response, we relax and benefit by having those chattering anxious thoughts get quieter almost instantly. It may sound like Dr. Jacobson put the cart before the horse, but this technique is well respected by therapists from many disciplines, simply because it works so well. It can benefit both the body and the brain. Some of the ways this exercise may benefit you if you do it several times weekly:

1. It can contribute to a general sense of calm and relaxation.
2. You can become more sensitive to—and more conscious of— the level of tension in your body. Most of us fail to realize that we are carrying tension until we feel the natural result— pain—especially in the neck or shoulders.

The progressive muscle relaxation exercise, as presented below, is a modification of the original one developed by Dr. Jacobson, but the process is essentially the same, as are the benefits. Please read over the instructions below. If you have any medical problems that preclude your doing any part of this, simply do the parts that you can. The first time you perform the exercise, you will have to open your eyes to read the steps. Once you know them, however, it is strongly recommended that you do the whole exercise with eyes closed so you can really focus on how it feels. Remember to give yourself plenty of time afterward to return to normal consciousness.

Let's begin:
Sit in a comfortable chair with both feet flat on the floor, or in a recliner.
Breathe at your own pace, naturally and easily.

Start with your forehead:
Tense the muscles in your forehead. Perhaps you can picture squeezing your eyebrows together or frowning tightly.
Hold the tension. Really feel it.
Then relax those muscles. Feel and really savor the difference.
Breathe in and out slowly. As you breathe out, enjoy the pleasant relaxed feeling in your muscles, allowing the pleasant feeling to increase throughout your body.

Next go to your eyes:

Close your eyes tightly. You might picture yourself in the shower. You don't want shampoo in your eyes, so you really tense those muscles.
Hold the tension. Really feel it.
Then relax those muscles. Feel the difference.
Breathe in and out slowly. As you breathe out, enjoy the pleasant relaxed feeling in your muscles, allowing the pleasant feeling to increase throughout your body.

Next your shoulders:

Pull your shoulders straight up toward your ears. Hold them there. Notice the tension.

Picture yourself monitoring this tension with an inner eye.

Then, release your shoulders. Relax. Notice how your shoulders feel when they are relaxed.

You may routinely carry the weight of your troubles around on your shoulders. This is a good time to release that weight.

Breathe in and out slowly. As you breathe out, enjoy the pleasant relaxed feeling in your muscles, allowing the pleasant feeling to increase throughout your body.

Next the arms:

Hold them straight out in front of you—about shoulder high.

Close your fists, but don't clench them. Push your fists forward, out in front of you so that the tension increases.

Your back should be pressing gently against the back of the chair.

Feel the tension. Let your internal monitor really notice how you feel.

Then, relax your arms and hands back into your lap. Notice how these muscles feel now.

Breathe in and out slowly. As you breathe out, enjoy the pleasant relaxed feeling in your muscles, allowing the pleasant feeling to increase throughout your body.

Next the abdomen:

Pull in your abdomen and hold the tension. Really feel the tension. Squeeze.

Then release the tension and feel the relaxation.

Breathe in and out slowly. As you breathe out, enjoy the pleasant relaxed feeling in your muscles, allowing the pleasant feeling to increase throughout your body.

Finally, the legs and feet:

Pick your feet up off the floor and hold them about one foot off the floor. (If you're in a recliner, just elevate them slightly).

Point your toes away from you. Increase the tension up your legs, in the feet, calves, thighs, all the way into the hips. Tighten.

Feel the tension. Really notice.

Then relax your feet and legs back to their original position. Notice how relaxation feels!

Breathe in and out slowly. As you breathe out, enjoy the pleasant relaxed feeling in your muscles, allowing the pleasant feeling to increase throughout your body.

For an extra bonus: After alternating tension and relaxation as described above, go back through the body and simply relax each of the areas. You will probably find it easier to really picture those muscle groups and to allow them to relax even more deeply.

(Jacobson, E. 1938. *Progressive Relaxation*. Chicago: University of Chicago Press.)

Note: You may also enjoy listening to this by going to the website: www.kendrabrownphd.com

Pause Button

Tool #11 Breathing for Relaxation: Using Nature's Way Enhanced

As with other relaxation and meditation exercises, I suggest that you find a quiet place away from electronic interruptions and other distractions. You shouldn't do any of these exercises when you are operating machinery. Allow yourself time afterward to return to regular life and full consciousness.

For this exercise, you will be asked to breathe deeply using your diaphragm. Two names for this type of breathing are *diaphragmatic breathing* and *abdominal breathing*. Whichever name you prefer—the result is that it interrupts the fight or flight response and promotes calm feelings and thinking. Diaphragmatic breathing is encouraged by many scientists who study behavioral medicine. Their research shows benefits in reducing anxiety and pain. There are numerous articles on abdominal breathing easily accessed through the Internet from leading universities and centers for integrative health.

In preparation for this exercise, it may be helpful to experience abdominal breathing. You can do this while sitting in a comfortable chair. Place one hand on your upper chest and the other hand below your rib cage (on your belly). As you inhale, the belly hand should rise. As you exhale, that hand will return to the original position. Your chest and shoulders should remain still. Don't hold your breath between inhaling and exhaling; simply follow a relaxed, rhythmic pattern that feels right for you. Now, let's get started:

> Sit either in a comfortable chair with both feet flat on the floor or in a recliner.
> Your hands should be resting comfortably in your lap, palms up.
> Close your eyes and begin breathing using your diaphragm, letting your belly rise and fall.
> Focus on the relaxation that follows.
> At this point, you are breathing as nature intended when you're not fearful.

What follows is the enhancement:

In this comfortable calm state, imagine that you have a part of yourself that does not judge or analyze—a part of yourself who can serve you as a best friend—simply noticing and listening. I'm calling that part of you the Accepting Self. This part allows you to feel safe. With the help of your new friend, you may allow thoughts and feelings to surface—nothing planned ahead of time, just whatever is there at this moment. In the safe embrace of your Accepting Self, you can listen to these thoughts and experience the feelings.

If a feeling or thought is disturbing, you simply return your focus to the diaphragmatic breathing and calm yourself again. You might be tempted to analyze or criticize some of the thoughts or feelings, but just let them come and go.

When you are ready, at just the right time for you, take just a couple more minutes to practice abdominal breathing, really focusing on the relaxation that may result. Then you may choose to return to your normal state of wakefulness and full consciousness.

This exercise may help you counter anxiety, and it can promote self-knowledge and valuable insights. You may also enjoy listening to this by going to the website: www.kendrabrownphd.com.

May 31

So he's back. No, that isn't quite precise. Ted is in my life again, but the place where we intersect isn't that same place it was months ago. I'm better at understanding who I am, who he is, and who we are together.

We literally bumped into each other as I came out of the gym a couple of days ago. Note to self: Always take a shower before exiting the gym because you never know who you might run into. I was flustered, but at least I smelled nice.

He seemed genuinely glad to see me, and I felt the same. After several cups of coffee at the shop around the corner, we were in love again, but differently. I don't feel desperate; I just feel delighted. I know now that it's wonderful to have him in my life, but he's not my whole life. That's too heavy a burden to put on someone. Hey, listen to me! I've learned a lot from Kathy.

One of the things I've learned, that I have to keep reminding myself, is her advice about a situation I think of as the prairie dog effect, where prairie dogs seem to pop up in unlikely parts of fields unexpectedly. Kathy warned me that when I encounter a tricky situation, my old self is very likely to come to the surface right away; in other words, I may revert to familiar behaviors, even if they're not especially good ones.

What I picture is going through life with past behaviors, like pesky prairie dogs, popping up in unexpected places, sort of like a game of whack-a-mole. I've learned that I don't have to hit them to get them back into their hole—I can observe them and choose how to deal with them.

It takes a conscious effort to remember the new behaviors until they become the familiar ones, Kathy says. The more you practice the new behaviors you've chosen, the more comfortable they become and the better you feel.

Hey, easier said than done, huh? If we could just be told these things a couple of times, memorize the words, and have them change how we act, the world would be great. But as I learned from reading all those books and magazines so many months ago, the words won't do it. You have to practice. In Kathy's words, you have to be "mindful."

She reminded me of the breathing exercises and meditation techniques she has shown me. She says these will help when I see those prairie dogs sticking up their heads and chattering in my direction. She says they will also help my new and improved behaviors become a deeper part of me so that they get way down in the marrow of my being.

I'm looking forward to it. I've come a long way in my journey to understand my own behaviors. I'm not going back to where I was.

I also think I'll spare Ted the knowledge that I did a PAC scan on him.

June 12

The more things change, the more they stay the same.

Of course, my mother was delighted that Ted and I are back together. "Maybe you've learned your lesson, and you'll treat him better," she said. Oh, no. Here we go again.

I felt the impulse to say things I would have regretted, but I used my relaxation tools instead. I could detach myself a bit to see that my mother was really expressing her own fears for me, and even though I found her remark to be totally insulting to both Ted and me, I realized that she was trapped in her own behaviors. I didn't have to go there. I could remain in my Adult ego state.

Well, almost. I had to just run—literally. I ran into the family room and acted oh so interested in whatever little game my nieces were playing. I still can't discuss personal situations rationally with my mother. Mom is still Mom, and even though I understand better, I still react. At least I've learned to remove myself from the situation when I feel overwhelmed, and I give myself a chance to reposition myself into an "Okay" frame of mind.

I asked Kathy about this, and she explained that sometimes people change in their behavior toward us once we change our behaviors, but not always. Yep, not always. I need to remember that I'm the one I can control, Kathy says. And really, that makes all the difference.

August 1

I've been using Kathy's meditations and breathing techniques for a while now, and I can feel the effect. I'm much more able to control myself when I feel those old behaviors start to come to the surface. Ever since I began to visualize them as chattering prairie dogs, I've been better able to confront them and choose the behaviors that make me feel good—the ones where I'm acting from my Adult ego state, feeling in charge of myself and my own reactions to people and situations.

If I had to say whether the therapy is working, I would point to the way people have been treating me. I've been doing much better at work, where I have become the go-to person when there are sticky situations that require some finesse. Me, the wrecking ball, the two hundred tons of sarcasm! I'm now the one who soothes and strategizes.

My sister and I are getting along so much better. I've been able to admit that I admire her, now that I'm not feeling so inadequate. Ironically, she's now been able to admit that she was actually jealous of me because of the freedom she thought I had in setting my own direction in life. Jealous! I was scared and confused, and she was jealous!

Ted is terrific. It's obvious that we're both enjoying ourselves, and I can't believe how much easier it is these days to negotiate our differences. I'm not sure what the future holds for us, but I'm loving the present moments.

And then there's Mother. Oh well, as they say, you can't win them all. This may be a work in progress for a very long time.

So where's the angst?

You know I couldn't lose it all that easily.

My biggest angst right now is over Kathy.

I went into this with the idea that I didn't want to be in full-time therapy for years, mostly because I knew I couldn't afford it. I was excited to find Kathy, who believed that I could have several sessions spaced out over a limited period of time and learn tools that would help me.

She says that we've arrived. Where? Surely not at a place where she can leave me! I'm having separation anxiety.

Of course, when I told her that she couldn't leave me in the forest this way, with wild beasts trolling the landscape and looking for a snack, she laughed.

"Remember the purpose of the tool kit," she said. "You know what you have to do, you have ways to describe behaviors using transactional analysis, and you understand the four life positions. You have meditation and breathing exercises to assist you, and you can always come back for a little retooling when necessary." The promise of retooling—that would be my lifeline.

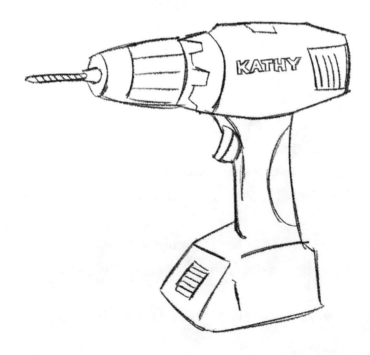

I realized that the most important tool that I used was Kathy. She wouldn't be flattered by this comparison, I'm sure, but I think of her as a power tool. She was the one who helped me understand my behaviors, and she was the one who enabled me to stock my tool kit with other tools that I can pull out whenever I need them.

So I'm still an apprentice at this. But I've got good tools, and I can come back for a refresher in how to use them from someone who really is a master craftsman.

I hope you build your own tool kit—I'll be too busy using my own to lend it to you. J

References and Suggested Reading

More about Transactional Analysis:

Berne, E. 1964. *Games People Play*. New York: Grove Press.

Ernst, F. 2008. *Transactional Analysis in the OK Corral: Grid for What's Happening*. Vallejo: Addresso' Set Publications.

Freed, A. and M. 1977. *TA for Kids (and grown-ups too)*. Torrance: Jalmar Press.

Harris, T. 1967. *I'm OK—You're OK*. New York: Harper & Row.

Stewart, I. and Joines, V. 2012. *TA Today*. Chapel Hill: Lifespace Publishing.

White, T. 1994. "Life Positions." *Transactional Analysis Journal* (24): 269–276.

More about Personality Types:

Jung, C. 1923. *Psychological Types or The Psychology of Individuation*. New York: Harcourt, Brace & Company.

Keirsey, D. and Bates, M. 1984. *Please Understand Me: Character and Temperament Types*. Green Valley Lake: Prometheus Nemesis Book Company.

Kroeger, O. and Thuesen, J. 1989. *Type Talk: The 16 Personality Types That Determine How We Live, Love, and Work*. New York: Dell Publishing Company.

Myers, I. and P. 1980. *Gifts Differing: Understanding Personality Type*. Mountain View: Davies- Black Publishing.

Meditations and Relaxation:

Jacobson, E. 1938. *Progressive Relaxation*. Chicago: University of Chicago Press.

Satir, V. 1995. *Meditations and Inspirations*. Berkeley: Celestial Arts.

Teasdale, J., Williams, M., and Segal, Z. 2014. *The Mindful Way Workbook*. New York: The Guilford Press.

Watt, T. 2012. *Mindfulness: A Practical Guide*. New York: MJF Books.

General:

Auerbach, J. 2013. *Irritating the Ones You Love*. Springville, Utah: Plain Sight Publishing.

Jampolsky, G. 1979. *Love Is Letting Go of Fear*. Berkeley: Celestial Arts.

Kelly, G. 1963. *The Psychology of Personal Constructs*. New York: W. W. Norton & Company.

About the Authors

Kendra T. Brown, Ph.D. is a licensed Psychologist in Stuart, Florida where she has enjoyed a thriving private practice for over twenty years. Her therapy is primarily solution oriented, working collaboratively with her clients, constructing strategies and techniques to help them achieve their goals. She is the author of: Eavesdropping: As Real Women Talk About the Gifts and Challenges of Aging (published by Rainbow Books in 2012 and currently in its second printing, available on <u>Amazon.com</u>). This book was born out of Brown's passion for empowering women of all ages. The lively discussions in Eavesdropping were re-creations of a group project she started in 2009, which continued for three years. Before earning her Ph.D. from the University of Memphis, she was a teacher in special education and the field director of human resources for a large company. Dr. Brown has lectured, taught and written in the fields of psychology, sports enhancement, human resources, and hypnosis. She continues to market her book through public speaking, appearances at libraries and book clubs, as a sponsor for local NPR, and through a monthly newsletter on her website: www.kendrabrownphd.com.

Patricia Austin Novak is a Public Relations professional, past president of The Florida Public Relations Association on the Treasure Coast, and recipient of the Communicator of the Year Award. She has an extensive career in public service and has been the marketing advisor for many of the larger organizations on Florida's Treasure Coast. Pat serves on the boards of several community non-profit organizations, including the local (four county) mental health center. She is an adjunct professor in writing and has long-term relationships with the local state university.